The Bravest Me

A Journey Through Fears and Dreams

Laura Lee

How Courage, Curiosity, and Compassion Shape Who We Are.

1 The Bravest Me: A Journey Through Fears and Dreams

2 The Bravest Me: A Journey Through Fears and Dreams

Copyright © 2024 by Laura Lee
All rights reserved. No part of this book may be reproduced or transmitted in any form or by any means, electronic or mechanical, including photocopying, recording, or any information storage and retrieval system, without the prior written permission of the author, except for the use of brief quotations in a book review or scholarly journal.

For information, please contact:
info@Lauxonpublishing.com
www.Lauxonpublishing.com

Disclaimer:
The content in this book is for informational purposes only and is not intended as a substitute for professional advice. The author and publisher shall not be liable for any damages arising from the use or misuse of the information contained herein.

PROLOGUE: THE JOURNEY BEGINS

Every great story has a beginning—a spark that ignites change, a whisper that dares us to move. For each of us, that whisper comes at a different time, maybe when we're a child dreaming big dreams, or maybe when we've grown and started to feel the edges of our world closing in. This book is about that spark, that whisper, that small yet powerful pull we feel deep within to become the bravest version of ourselves.

The Bravest Me: A Journey Through Fears and Dreams isn't about fearlessness. It's about the courage to walk through our fears, to hold them close and understand them, and ultimately, to grow through them. We aren't here to reject fear or wish it away; rather, we're here to make it our teacher, a companion in the journey to something bigger.

The journey begins with a simple but powerful truth: courage, curiosity, and compassion shape who we are. They are the truest parts of ourselves that guide us, help us find meaning, and allow us to connect more deeply with the world and people around us. In courage, we face challenges that might have seemed impossible; in curiosity, we explore possibilities beyond our wildest dreams; in compassion, we find the strength to forgive, to heal, and to love—ourselves and others.

As we start this journey, I invite you to bring along your fears and dreams, your doubts and hopes, and every part of you that wonders what else might be possible. Each chapter will take us further down the path, from facing fears to uncovering dreams, from timid curiosity to daring courage, from self-judgment to self-compassion. You may find that along the way, some parts of you are ready to grow and change, while others need more time, more patience. And that's okay. Growth, like courage, is not about speed; it's about showing up and daring to try.

Imagine yourself at the start of a trail winding through unknown territory. You feel the butterflies of anticipation mixed with a touch of fear. Ahead of you, the road is unclear, but each step forward reveals something new, something meaningful. As you walk, remember this: you are not alone, and every small step toward courage, every moment of curiosity, every act of kindness—these shape who you are becoming.

This is your journey, and within these pages, you will find encouragement to walk at your own pace, to feel all that you need to feel, and to become the bravest you. So take a breath, open your heart, and let the journey begin. The bravest version of you is waiting, ready to be discovered.

Welcome to *The Bravest Me*.

TABLE OF CONTENTS

Part 1: Embracing Fear (Chapters 1-10)

Chapter 1: The Seeds of Fear

An introduction to fear and its roots. Readers explore the nature of fears they inherited from society, family, and personal experiences, setting the foundation for a journey of self-discovery.

Chapter 2: The Anatomy of Fear

This chapter dives into the science and psychology of fear, helping readers understand the biological responses to threats, both real and imagined.

Chapter 3: Shadows of Doubt

Explores the effect of self-doubt on personal growth. Readers learn to recognize internal voices that hold them back and begin reframing negative self-talk.

Chapter 4: Breaking the Chains of Past Trauma

A sensitive chapter on addressing past traumas that anchor fears. This chapter introduces tools for gentle healing and self-compassion, setting the stage for resilience.

Chapter 5: The Masks We Wear

Explores how fear shapes identities and forces people to wear "masks." Readers are encouraged to shed these masks, discovering the authentic self hidden underneath.

Chapter 6: Facing the Fear of Rejection

Readers confront one of the most common fears: rejection. This chapter emphasizes how embracing vulnerability and authenticity allows people to find real acceptance.

Chapter 7: Taking a Step into the Unknown

Discusses the importance of stepping outside comfort zones, with practical strategies for handling the anxiety of new and uncertain situations.

Chapter 8: Finding Stillness Amidst Fear

Introduces mindfulness techniques, helping readers pause and center themselves during moments of fear.

Chapter 9: The Art of Self-Compassion

A chapter that encourages readers to practice self-compassion, especially when facing fears. This practice becomes a foundation for growth and resilience.

Chapter 10: Building Courage One Small Step at a Time

This chapter emphasizes the value of incremental courage, showing that small acts of bravery can have a big impact on the journey.

Part 2: Cultivating Curiosity (Chapters 11-20)

Chapter 11: The Spark of Curiosity

The shift from fear to curiosity is introduced here. Readers learn how curiosity can transform fear into wonder, opening doors to new possibilities.

Chapter 12: Unpacking Childhood Dreams

A reflective chapter where readers revisit dreams and aspirations from their youth, examining how these dreams shaped them and whether they still hold power.

Chapter 13: Asking the Right Questions

An exploration of the power of questions. Readers learn how to ask themselves constructive questions that lead to meaningful answers and insights.

Chapter 14: The Magic of Learning Something New

Embracing the joy of learning, this chapter encourages readers to try a new skill, hobby, or interest as a form of self-exploration.

Chapter 15: Curiosity About Others

Explores empathy and understanding through curiosity about others' experiences. Readers are invited to expand their worldview by engaging with different perspectives.

Chapter 16: Embracing the Unknown with Open Arms

Discusses how curiosity and openness toward the unknown can make challenges feel like adventures instead of obstacles.

Chapter 17: Turning Setbacks into Stepping Stones

Explores resilience in the face of setbacks. This chapter shows how curiosity allows readers to view failure as a teacher, finding lessons in even the hardest moments.

Chapter 18: Curiosity as a Path to Self-Discovery

This chapter provides introspective exercises for self-reflection, encouraging readers to uncover new layers of their identity and desires.

Chapter 19: Fueling Dreams with Curiosity

Discusses the importance of dreaming big and nurturing aspirations with genuine curiosity. This chapter emphasizes self-belief as the root of possibility.

Chapter 20: The Courage to Question the Status Quo

Encourages readers to critically examine societal expectations and norms, asking them to think about how their dreams align (or don't) with traditional paths.

Part 3: Nurturing Compassion (Chapters 21-30)

Chapter 21: The Power of Self-Compassion

Circles back to the concept of self-compassion in a more profound way, examining how it supports healing and personal growth, especially when courage falters.

Chapter 22: Compassionate Connections

Highlights the role of compassion in relationships. Readers learn about active listening, empathy, and how caring for others nurtures their own journey.

Chapter 23: The Strength in Vulnerability

Examines vulnerability as a strength. Through stories and examples, readers see how honesty with themselves and others fosters true connections and courage.

Chapter 24: Forgiveness as a Path to Freedom

This chapter explores forgiveness as a liberating practice, particularly in terms of self-forgiveness. It demonstrates how forgiveness frees people from the weight of past mistakes.

Chapter 25: Compassion in Times of Fear

Readers explore how compassion toward others can help them overcome fear. This chapter provides real-world examples of bravery inspired by empathy.

Chapter 26: Finding Joy in Helping Others

An inspiring chapter that highlights the role of altruism in personal growth. Readers are encouraged to find ways to help others, discovering joy and fulfillment.

Chapter 27: Building a Support Network

Discusses the importance of creating a network of like-minded, supportive individuals. Readers are guided in how to seek out and nurture relationships that inspire bravery.

Chapter 28: Choosing Kindness Every Day

Shows the value of everyday kindness, even in small acts. Readers are encouraged to view kindness as a reflection of courage and as a practice to uplift both themselves and others.

Chapter 29: Living Authentically with Purpose

This chapter helps readers align their actions and values with their purpose. The courage to live authentically is framed as a lifelong practice that honors both dreams and fears.

Chapter 30: The Bravest Me - Embracing the Journey Forward

A reflective conclusion that celebrates the courage, curiosity, and compassion readers have developed. This chapter empowers them to continue their journey with open hearts and minds, shaping a future they believe in.

13 The Bravest Me: A Journey Through Fears and Dreams

14 The Bravest Me: A Journey Through Fears and Dreams

PART 1: EMBRACING FEAR (CHAPTERS 1-10)

1
THE SEEDS OF FEAR

Fear is universal. It's in the pulse that quickens, the stomach that churns, the hesitation that halts us. It has been with us since the beginning, woven tightly into our survival instincts. And yet, fear is so much more than a biological response—it is a complex, multifaceted part of us that shapes who we are, often without our realizing it.

When we begin to peel back the layers of our fears, we discover that many of them have been planted deep within us over the course of our lives. Some of these fears feel almost inherited, passed down from generation to generation, while others come from our personal experiences, relationships, and the messages we've absorbed from the world around us. Fear, it seems, is a tapestry—one we often don't see until we take the time to look at each individual thread.

In this chapter, we'll examine the roots of fear. Not to eliminate it or cast it aside but to understand where it comes from and what it means. Just as a tree's roots reach deep into the soil to hold it steady and draw nourishment, so too do our fears reach into our past, our identity, and our culture, grounding us in what we know, whether it's comforting or not. To truly begin our journey toward courage, we must start here—at the source, with the seeds of fear.

Inherited Fear: The Echoes of Our Past

Some of our earliest fears are those we didn't choose. They come to us from family members, subtly shaping the way we see the world. A child raised by parents who fear the unknown may grow up wary of change. A parent's anxiety over financial security may pass to a child who, without understanding why, grows up fearing poverty or instability.

These inherited fears are a legacy, often unintentionally handed down. They're shaped by generations who lived through their own challenges—war, hardship, loss. Sometimes, the fears our parents or grandparents held were essential for their survival. But as times change, we often find that these old fears no longer serve us; they hold us back more than they protect us. The question then becomes: can we honor where these fears came from without allowing them to control us?

Societal Fears: The Pressures of Conformity and Judgment

From the moment we're born, society begins shaping our understanding of what is safe and what is risky, what is acceptable and what is not. We're given a set of rules that tell us how to belong, how to avoid rejection. Some of these rules protect us, but others create limits that stifle our true selves. Society tells us to fear failure, to fear rejection, to fear standing out too much or standing up too boldly.

These societal fears are often the hardest to see because they're so deeply embedded in our culture and our minds. They become "normal" to us, invisible boundaries we rarely question. Yet they dictate much of our behavior. Why do we fear trying something new? Why do we worry about what others will think? We often find that behind these questions are deeply ingrained beliefs that society has woven into our identities over the years. To be brave, we must start by identifying these fears and challenging the ways they shape our choices.

Personal Fears: The Experiences that Shape Us

The most personal fears are those born of our own experiences. These fears are unique to each of us, shaped by our life stories—the moments of vulnerability, the instances of pain, the times when we felt our safety or our hearts were at risk. These are the fears that come from real-life scars, both physical and emotional, and they're often the most difficult to face.

Perhaps you experienced rejection when you took a chance on love, or perhaps you faced judgment when you shared your dreams. These fears are specific, layered, and powerful because they're rooted in real memories. They remind us of our humanity and the desire to protect ourselves from pain. Yet as much as they protect us, they can also limit us. In facing these fears, we must ask ourselves: can we honor our past hurts without letting them define our future?

Reflection: Tracing the Roots

Understanding our fears begins with awareness. By seeing them for what they are—threads from our family, culture, and life experiences—we can begin to unravel them. This isn't about rejecting our fears; it's about understanding them with empathy and clarity.

In this moment, take a pause. Reflect on the fears you carry. Consider writing them down, tracing their roots. Which ones feel inherited, as if they belong to someone else? Which come from society's expectations? Which ones are deeply personal, a reflection of your own experiences?

As we journey through this book, we'll revisit these fears with fresh eyes, taking each one and understanding it a little more. This chapter isn't about "getting over" fear or making it disappear. Instead, it's about beginning a relationship with fear that allows us to learn from it, to transform it into something that no longer controls us but rather accompanies us on our journey.

Remember that fear, like courage, is a part of us. It's a teacher if we allow it to be, a mirror that reflects what we value and care about most. And in the end, it can be a guide. By understanding fear's roots, we create the foundation for self-discovery and growth —one that will lead us down the path toward the bravest version of ourselves.

2
THE ANATOMY OF FEAR

Fear is an ancient part of who we are, a primal response designed to protect us from danger. It sharpens our senses, triggers a flood of chemicals in our bodies, and heightens our awareness, all to help us survive. But in modern life, fear often responds not only to actual threats but also to imagined ones—problems and possibilities that exist only in our minds. When we understand the science of fear, we can begin to see it as both a helpful ally and, at times, an overprotective guardian. This awareness is the first step toward learning how to respond to fear in ways that empower, rather than limit, us.

In this chapter, we'll explore the fascinating anatomy of fear. From the way it manifests in our brains to how it affects our bodies, we'll see how this complex emotion has evolved and how we can work with it to help us grow. By learning how fear functions, we're better equipped to recognize when it's warning us of a real threat—and when it's holding us back from fulfilling our potential.

The Brain on Fear: The Amygdala and the Fight-or-Flight Response

Fear begins in a small, almond-shaped structure in the brain called the amygdala, located deep within the temporal lobe. The amygdala acts as an alarm system, constantly scanning our environment for threats. When it perceives something dangerous, it sends out a distress signal to the rest of the brain, particularly to the hypothalamus, which initiates the body's fight-or-flight response.

This response is immediate and powerful. It's what allowed our ancestors to survive in a world filled with predators and other life-threatening dangers. In an instant, our brains can go from calm to high alert, flooding our bodies with stress hormones like adrenaline and cortisol. Our heart rate quickens, our breathing speeds up, and our muscles tense, all in preparation to either confront or escape from danger.

But the amygdala's sense of threat is not always perfect. It doesn't distinguish between physical dangers, like a wild animal, and social or emotional threats, like public speaking or fear of failure. Our brains and bodies respond in similar ways to both real and imagined threats, making it easy for fear to become a frequent, even daily, part of our lives. Recognizing that fear is often a reflexive, automatic response helps us to see that not every fearful feeling signals real danger.

The Role of the Prefrontal Cortex: Reasoning and Reassurance

Fortunately, we aren't at the mercy of our amygdala alone. The brain also has the prefrontal cortex, the region responsible for reasoning, decision-making, and self-control. This part of the brain helps us assess the situation more rationally. When we feel fear, our prefrontal cortex can "step in" and evaluate the actual level of threat. It can ask questions like: *Is this fear grounded in reality? Am I actually in danger, or is my mind imagining the worst possible outcome?*

The prefrontal cortex allows us to bring awareness to our fear. When we pause, take a deep breath, and examine our fears, we're engaging this part of the brain, which helps calm the amygdala's response. By working with both the amygdala and the prefrontal cortex, we can learn to balance instinct with reason, helping us to make choices that are neither impulsively driven by fear nor recklessly dismissive of it.

The Body's Response: How Fear Affects Us Physically

Our experience of fear isn't only in the mind; it manifests in the body as well. When we're afraid, our bodies undergo a series of physical changes, often in an instant. Our pupils dilate to let in more light, making us more alert. Our heart rate increases to pump blood to our muscles, preparing us to take action. We may feel a tightness in our chest or a lump in our throat, common responses to the flood of adrenaline coursing through us.

In small doses, these physical responses can actually be helpful. A slight elevation in adrenaline can make us more focused, alert, and motivated. But if we experience these effects too frequently or too intensely, it can take a toll on our health. Chronic fear, even of non-life-threatening situations, can lead to ongoing stress, which weakens the immune system, strains the heart, and affects sleep, memory, and mood. Understanding how fear affects our bodies allows us to recognize the importance of managing it, both for mental clarity and physical well-being.

Real vs. Imagined Threats: The Power of the Mind

One of the most fascinating aspects of fear is how easily the mind can blur the line between what is real and what is imagined. We don't need an immediate physical threat to feel afraid; often, just imagining a worst-case scenario is enough to trigger the same fear response as if we were truly in danger. This tendency is why fears of the future—worries about things that haven't happened and may never happen—can affect us so powerfully.

When we imagine something fearful, our brains and bodies respond as if it's happening in real time. This is a phenomenon known as "anticipatory anxiety." The mind projects a future scenario, the amygdala senses a threat, and the body reacts.

Understanding this process helps us see that much of our fear is not about present reality; it's about possible outcomes that our minds have created. This awareness gives us the power to question our fears, asking, *Is this fear based on what is actually happening now, or on what I imagine might happen?*

Tools for Calming the Fear Response

The knowledge of how fear works biologically gives us the foundation to begin working with it more effectively. There are tools we can use to manage our responses, grounding ourselves when fear begins to take over.

Breathing Exercises: Deep, slow breathing helps signal to the brain that we are not in immediate danger, which calms the amygdala and activates the body's relaxation response. Taking a few deep breaths can help us shift from fight-or-flight mode to a more relaxed state.

Mindfulness and Meditation: Mindfulness allows us to observe our fear without judgment, creating a space where we can acknowledge it without becoming overwhelmed. Meditation strengthens the prefrontal cortex over time, helping us approach fear with a calmer, more reasoned perspective.

Reframing Thoughts: By consciously reframing fearful thoughts, we engage the prefrontal cortex to think critically about what we're afraid of. For example, instead of thinking, "I can't do this; I'll fail," we can try, "This is challenging, but I'm capable of learning and adapting." This practice weakens fear's hold and allows courage to take root.

Gradual Exposure: Facing fear gradually, in small, manageable doses, teaches the brain that the feared situation is not as threatening as it may feel. This method, known as "exposure therapy," helps the amygdala learn to "calm down" in situations it might initially perceive as dangerous.

Reflection: Listening to Fear's Messages

Fear isn't something to eliminate. It's a part of us, a messenger that, when approached with understanding, can guide us toward growth and self-awareness. Knowing the biology of fear gives us the chance to work with it in a healthier, more productive way. As we move forward, we'll learn that fear is not something to be ashamed of or frustrated by; rather, it's a tool that helps us understand our vulnerabilities and, ultimately, our strength.

Take a moment now to reflect on a recent experience where you felt afraid. Think about the physical sensations, the thoughts that went through your mind, and how you reacted. Ask yourself: was this fear protecting me, or was it responding to an imagined threat? This exercise is a first step in becoming more aware of fear's role in our lives.

By understanding the anatomy of fear, we gain a better grasp of how to respond to it. We're not trying to live without fear; rather, we're learning to live with it, guiding it rather than letting it control us. In the next chapter, we'll explore how self-doubt often intertwines with fear, creating a cycle of hesitation that can hold us back from fully living. But with each insight, we're moving closer to understanding the full picture of what it means to be brave.

3

SHADOWS OF DOUBT

Doubt is a quiet yet powerful force. Unlike the rush of fear, which can flood us with adrenaline, doubt seeps in slowly, almost unnoticed, until it becomes a familiar presence. While fear often signals an external threat, doubt whispers from within. It questions our abilities, our worth, and our potential, casting a shadow over our dreams and ambitions. Left unchecked, self-doubt can hold us back from becoming who we're meant to be.

In this chapter, we'll explore the origins of self-doubt and its effect on our lives. We'll look at how these voices of doubt—often internalized messages from others or beliefs shaped by our experiences—limit our growth and prevent us from taking risks. Most importantly, we'll begin the work of challenging and reframing this negative self-talk, transforming it into encouragement that empowers us to move forward.

The Roots of Self-Doubt: Where Does It Come From?

Doubt rarely appears out of nowhere. Most often, it's rooted in past experiences, relationships, and societal messages that have shaped how we see ourselves. It's the memory of a critical teacher, the words of a parent who warned against taking risks, the sting of a past failure, or the internalization of cultural expectations that dictate who we "should" be. These influences may have been well-intentioned, meant to protect us from disappointment or rejection, but over time, they form a chorus of voices that question our every move.

For many, self-doubt becomes a defense mechanism—a way of avoiding pain by convincing ourselves not to try in the first place. "Why risk failing?" it asks. "Better to stay where you are than to reach too high." And while this logic may have once helped us survive rejection or hurt, it ultimately limits us, creating a cycle of self-criticism that keeps us from growth.

The Inner Critic: Recognizing the Voices That Hold Us Back

One of the most common manifestations of self-doubt is the "inner critic." This voice in our heads can be harsh, judgmental, and relentless, telling us we're not good enough, smart enough, or capable enough to pursue what we want. The inner critic thrives on perfectionism, comparing us to an ideal that no one can achieve. It's quick to point out mistakes and slow to recognize accomplishments.

Often, the inner critic sounds like a blend of voices we've heard throughout our lives: an overly critical parent, a demanding coach, or the weight of societal expectations. It feeds on our vulnerabilities and amplifies them, convincing us that any mistake or imperfection is evidence that we're not worthy. By learning to identify this voice, we take the first step in lessening its power over us.

The Imposter Syndrome: "Who Am I to…?"

Self-doubt often surfaces in the form of imposter syndrome, a pervasive feeling that we're somehow "faking it" and that it's only a matter of time before others realize we're not as capable as they think. People who struggle with imposter syndrome feel as though they don't truly deserve their achievements. They may downplay their successes, attributing them to luck rather than skill, and live with the constant fear of being "exposed."

Imposter syndrome is particularly common when we step outside our comfort zones, as it taps into our fear of failure and rejection.

Many talented, successful individuals live with imposter syndrome, despite evidence of their abilities. Recognizing that these feelings are common can be the first step toward challenging them. By acknowledging that self-doubt is often a sign we're growing and stretching ourselves, we can begin to view it as an opportunity for growth rather than a barrier.

The Cycle of Self-Doubt: How It Holds Us Back

The cycle of self-doubt can be challenging to break because it's self-reinforcing. When we doubt ourselves, we hesitate to take action. That hesitation often leads to inaction or to a half-hearted attempt, which then reinforces the belief that we aren't capable. Over time, this cycle builds a "comfort zone" around us—a boundary that feels safe because it's familiar, even if it's not where we truly want to be.

This cycle is often rooted in negative self-talk, the repetitive thoughts that tell us what we can't do or shouldn't try. For example, thoughts like "I'll never be able to do that," or "Others are so much better than me" create self-imposed limits. They become the shadows of doubt, clouding our confidence and convincing us to settle for less than we're capable of.

Reframing Self-Doubt: Turning Criticism into Encouragement

Reframing negative self-talk is one of the most effective ways to combat self-doubt. This process involves actively challenging critical thoughts and transforming them into supportive ones. Instead of thinking, "I'm not good enough to do this," we might reframe it to, "I'm learning and growing with each step I take." This shift doesn't deny our doubts; it simply reshapes them into thoughts that are more helpful and constructive.

Consider treating your inner critic like a well-meaning but misinformed friend. The next time a negative thought arises, pause and ask yourself, "What would I say to a friend who's feeling this way?" It's often easier to be compassionate and encouraging with others than with ourselves, but practicing this perspective allows us to reframe self-doubt with a more balanced view.

Another helpful strategy is to look for evidence that challenges our doubt. For instance, if you catch yourself thinking, "I can't do this," consider any evidence from your past that shows you can or have done similar things. Maybe you once accomplished something difficult or handled a challenge successfully. By reminding ourselves of our strengths and abilities, we counterbalance the voice of doubt.

The Power of Self-Compassion: Making Space for Growth

Self-compassion is one of the most effective antidotes to self-doubt. It means treating ourselves with the same kindness, patience, and understanding that we would offer to someone we care about. Instead of criticizing ourselves for feeling uncertain, we acknowledge that self-doubt is a normal part of growth. We remind ourselves that everyone feels this way sometimes and that mistakes and setbacks don't define us—they are simply part of the learning process.

By practicing self-compassion, we make space for growth and resilience. Rather than letting self-doubt stop us, we approach it with curiosity, asking ourselves what it might be teaching us about our values, goals, and aspirations. In this way, we transform self-doubt from an obstacle into a stepping stone, a reminder that we are capable of so much more than our doubts suggest.

Reflection: Challenging the Shadows

In this moment, take a few deep breaths and think about a goal or dream you've been holding back on due to self-doubt. Notice the thoughts and feelings that come up. Write them down if you can. What is your inner critic saying? What doubts are surfacing?

Now, try to reframe these thoughts. Instead of thinking, "I'll never be able to do this," try, "This may be challenging, but I'm willing to take it one step at a time." Instead of "I'm not good enough," consider, "I am learning, and I'll grow with each experience."

With each reframed thought, you're reshaping the way you see yourself and your potential. You're allowing self-doubt to be a part of the journey, but not the one in control. This work is not easy, and it may take time. But each small step you take moves you closer to the bravest version of yourself, a version that can coexist with doubt without being defined by it.

As we move forward, remember that self-doubt is natural. It's a sign that we care about what we're pursuing, that we're reaching for something meaningful. In the next chapter, we'll explore the role of courage—how it doesn't require us to banish fear and doubt but instead allows us to act in spite of them. Together, we're building a foundation for growth and resilience, one thought and one step at a time.

4
BREAKING THE CHAINS OF PAST TRAUMA

Trauma has a profound impact on our lives. It can live within us like an anchor, silently influencing how we see ourselves and the world. Our past traumas often become hidden drivers of fear, self-doubt, and hesitation. They can leave us feeling vulnerable, unsafe, and unworthy, shaping the way we respond to new situations, even if we're no longer in harm's way.

Healing from trauma is not about erasing the past; it's about reclaiming our sense of safety, trust, and self-worth. It's about finding ways to gently let go of what no longer serves us, creating space for courage and resilience to grow. This chapter will explore how trauma impacts our minds and bodies, and introduce tools for beginning the journey of healing with self-compassion and patience.

Understanding Trauma: The Roots of Fear and Vulnerability

Trauma is any experience that overwhelms our ability to cope and leaves a lasting impact on our sense of safety and self. It's not only severe events like abuse or violence that cause trauma; even situations that may seem minor to others can leave a deep impression, depending on our age, resilience, and emotional support at the time.

When we experience trauma, our brains respond by heightening their focus on survival. The amygdala, which detects danger, becomes hyperactive, causing us to feel "on edge" or reactive to any potential threats, even if they're minor or imagined. For those with past trauma, normal life events can sometimes trigger intense fear, anxiety, or a sense of helplessness, as if they're reliving the original event. Understanding that trauma is a learned response—one meant to protect us—helps us approach it with empathy rather than frustration.

Trauma also impacts our beliefs about ourselves. We may internalize feelings of guilt, shame, or worthlessness, thinking that we somehow deserved what happened or that we're defined by it. Recognizing these beliefs as remnants of the trauma, rather than truths, is essential in breaking free from its chains. We can begin to see ourselves not as people defined by what happened to us but as individuals capable of growth and healing.

The Mind-Body Connection: How Trauma Lives Within Us

One of the most profound ways trauma affects us is through the mind-body connection. When we experience something traumatic, our bodies respond by storing these memories not only as thoughts but as sensations. It's common for people with past trauma to feel tightness, pain, or unease in their bodies, particularly when they're reminded of the event.

Our bodies often "hold" the emotional and physical tension from trauma. In a way, this tension is our body's attempt to protect us from future harm, a kind of armor we wear to guard ourselves. But while this armor may protect us initially, over time it can weigh us down, making us feel disconnected from ourselves and others. Becoming aware of how trauma lives in the body allows us to approach healing in a way that honors both the mind and the physical sensations.

The Power of Self-Compassion: Healing Gently and Patiently

Healing from trauma is a deeply personal journey, one that often requires patience, kindness, and understanding. Self-compassion is a powerful tool for those carrying the weight of past trauma, as it helps us hold space for our pain without judgment. Trauma often creates feelings of shame and guilt, which can lead us to believe that we're "broken" or "flawed." Self-compassion reminds us that pain is a human experience and that we deserve to heal and feel whole.

Practicing self-compassion may involve simple affirmations or small acts of kindness toward ourselves. For example, when painful memories resurface, we might say, "This feeling is temporary, and I am safe now," or "It's okay to feel what I'm feeling. I'm here for myself." We begin to cultivate a gentle, caring inner voice that counteracts the harshness trauma can leave behind.

Tools for Healing: Beginning the Process

Healing from trauma is a journey that doesn't have to be traveled alone. Often, we benefit from working with mental health professionals, support groups, or other trusted people who can provide guidance and understanding. Here are a few gentle tools that can support us in addressing trauma's impact:

Grounding Techniques: When trauma-related thoughts or sensations arise, grounding can help bring us back to the present moment. Techniques like feeling the texture of an object, focusing on the sounds around us, or practicing deep breathing can help calm the nervous system. This process reminds our bodies that we're safe and that the past event is not happening in the present.

Mindful Body Awareness: Trauma often causes disconnection from the body. Practicing mindful body awareness—scanning our bodies to notice sensations without judgment—can help rebuild a sense of presence and safety within ourselves. Start by focusing on one area of the body at a time, noticing where you might be holding tension or unease, and gently relaxing those areas as much as possible.

Journaling and Expression: Writing about our experiences, feelings, or thoughts related to trauma can provide a safe outlet for processing emotions. Journaling is a way to externalize our pain, making it something we can observe from a distance rather than feeling trapped by it. Over time, journaling may help us to identify patterns, beliefs, and recurring fears, allowing us to see our growth as we work through these experiences.

Therapeutic Support: Engaging with a therapist or counselor trained in trauma can be transformative. Therapies like EMDR (Eye Movement Desensitization and Reprocessing), somatic therapy, and cognitive behavioral therapy are often used to help individuals work through trauma safely. A supportive professional can help us understand our trauma, create coping strategies, and gently guide us through the healing process.

Resilience: Transforming Trauma into Strength

Healing from trauma doesn't mean we "erase" the past. Instead, it allows us to build resilience—a strength that comes from surviving something difficult and emerging wiser, more compassionate, and more self-aware. Resilience is the ability to move forward despite setbacks, and it can transform how we see ourselves. With each step of healing, we begin to feel more capable of facing life's challenges and more confident in our ability to thrive.

Trauma may shape parts of us, but it does not define our future. When we break the chains of past trauma, we open ourselves up to new possibilities and experiences, ones that were once shadowed by fear. Resilience doesn't mean we forget our pain; it means we allow ourselves to move forward with a sense of hope and purpose, choosing to create a life that reflects our strength rather than our suffering.

Reflection: Embracing Self-Compassion in the Healing Journey

As you read this chapter, consider the areas in your life where past trauma may still hold you back. Are there certain situations, memories, or emotions that trigger fear or self-doubt? Reflect on how you respond to these feelings—do you judge yourself or push the feelings away, or do you allow yourself to feel them?

In this moment, take a few deep breaths. Picture yourself as someone deserving of patience, kindness, and healing. Imagine what you would say to a loved one if they were carrying the pain you carry, and offer those same words to yourself. Remind yourself that healing is a journey, and that it's okay to go at your own pace.

As we continue forward, remember that your resilience is already within you, and each step you take is a testament to your strength. In the next chapter, we'll explore how embracing vulnerability can empower us, helping us build deeper connections and live more authentically. Healing from trauma is not the end; it's the beginning of a life defined by courage and compassion.

5
THE MASKS WE WEAR

For much of our lives, we learn to adapt to the expectations and judgments of others. We develop different "masks"—versions of ourselves that feel safe, acceptable, or likable to those around us. These masks help us navigate society, avoid judgment, and sometimes even protect ourselves from rejection or vulnerability. But over time, these masks can weigh us down, obscuring our authentic selves and trapping us in identities that may no longer reflect who we truly are.

In this chapter, we'll explore the ways in which fear shapes our identities and how the masks we wear are often born from a desire to fit in or be "good enough." We'll also take steps to peel back these layers, uncovering the parts of ourselves we may have hidden away, and reconnecting with our most authentic selves.

The Origins of Our Masks: Adapting to Belong

As children, we're naturally curious and unfiltered. We express ourselves freely, without hesitation. But as we grow, we begin to notice the expectations of our families, friends, and society. We learn that certain behaviors, thoughts, or appearances are more acceptable than others. To gain acceptance and avoid criticism, we begin to shape ourselves around these expectations, hiding the parts that don't "fit" and accentuating those that do.

These masks can take many forms. For some, it might be the "perfectionist" mask, always striving to be flawless and earn approval. For others, it might be the "people-pleaser" mask, putting others' needs above their own to avoid conflict or rejection. Still others may wear the "tough" mask, concealing vulnerability behind a facade of strength. While these masks help us survive in certain situations, they also prevent us from living authentically, leaving us feeling disconnected from who we really are.

Fear as the Designer: How We Craft Our Masks

Fear plays a significant role in shaping these masks. We fear rejection, failure, or being seen as inadequate. We worry that if we show our true selves, we might not be loved or accepted. And so, we craft these identities—versions of ourselves we believe others will value, even if they don't align with our own values and needs.

For example, the fear of failure might lead someone to present themselves as a high-achieving perfectionist, never allowing themselves to make mistakes or show vulnerability. The fear of judgment might lead another to hide parts of their personality that they feel are "different" or "unacceptable." And while these identities help us feel safer in the moment, they often prevent us from experiencing the deep connections and fulfillment that come from living as our true selves.

The Cost of Wearing Masks: Disconnect and Self-Doubt

The masks we wear protect us from external judgment, but they also create an internal conflict. When we hide parts of ourselves, we lose touch with our own needs, desires, and values. This disconnect can lead to self-doubt, as we begin to wonder who we really are and what we genuinely want out of life. Living behind a mask can be exhausting, and it often leads to feelings of isolation and emptiness, even when we're surrounded by others.

Over time, the weight of these masks can feel unbearable. We may feel as though we're living someone else's life, constantly performing for others rather than honoring our own truths. The cost of wearing these masks is high, and the price we pay is often a sense of inner fulfillment and peace. By beginning to peel back these layers, we open ourselves up to the possibility of connection, self-acceptance, and authentic joy.

Shedding the Masks: Steps to Embrace the Authentic Self

Letting go of our masks is a gradual process. It requires courage, self-compassion, and patience. Here are a few steps to help us begin the journey of embracing our authentic selves:

Identify Your Masks: Start by reflecting on the different "roles" or "personas" you take on in different areas of your life. What are the qualities or behaviors you exaggerate or hide to fit in? Consider the situations where you feel the need to act a certain way to feel accepted. For example, do you feel the need to be "perfect" at work, or to always be cheerful around friends?

Acknowledge the Fear Behind the Mask: Each mask is often tied to a specific fear. Maybe it's the fear of rejection, the fear of failure, or the fear of being judged. By identifying the fears that fuel your masks, you begin to understand why you created them. This awareness is essential, as it allows you to approach these fears with compassion rather than judgment.

Practice Self-Compassion and Patience: Letting go of these masks can be scary and uncomfortable. Remind yourself that this is a gradual process and that you don't need to shed all your masks at once. Self-compassion is key here. Treat yourself with kindness as you explore parts of yourself that may have been hidden for a long time.

Take Small Steps to Show Up Authentically: Start by expressing your authentic self in small ways. This could be sharing an honest opinion, allowing yourself to say "no" when something doesn't align with your values, or showing vulnerability by asking for help when you need it. Each small act of authenticity helps build confidence and trust in yourself.

Surround Yourself with Supportive People: It's easier to be authentic when we feel safe and accepted. Seek out relationships with people who support and appreciate you for who you are. True friends encourage us to be ourselves, and they don't demand us to fit into a particular mold.

The Freedom of Authenticity: Living Without the Masks

Living authentically is freeing. Without the weight of pretense, we can move through life with a sense of ease and confidence. Our relationships become richer, as people connect with us for who we really are, rather than who we're pretending to be. Authenticity opens the door to deeper self-respect, as we align our actions with our true values rather than conforming to external expectations.

Embracing our authentic selves also allows us to experience vulnerability as a strength. When we show up as we are—flaws, fears, and all—we create space for genuine connection and trust. We begin to attract people and opportunities that resonate with our true selves, creating a life that feels more fulfilling and meaningful.

Reflection: Embracing Your True Self

As you begin the journey of shedding your masks, take a moment to reflect on who you are at your core. What values are most important to you? What brings you joy and fulfillment? Write down these reflections as a way of reconnecting with your authentic self.

Imagine the feeling of living a life free from the masks you've worn. Picture yourself moving through the world as your truest self, confident in your values and open to new connections. Hold on to this vision as you continue forward, knowing that each step toward authenticity brings you closer to a life of deeper meaning and freedom.

In the next chapter, we'll explore the role of vulnerability in personal growth. Just as shedding masks requires us to show up authentically, embracing vulnerability helps us navigate life with courage and openness. Together, these qualities create a path to resilience and self-acceptance, helping us shape a life that is fully and truly our own.

6
FACING THE FEAR OF REJECTION

Rejection is one of the most deeply rooted fears humans experience. From our earliest days, we seek connection, belonging, and acceptance. Rejection threatens those needs and can make us feel isolated, inadequate, or even unloved. Whether it's in relationships, careers, or creative pursuits, the fear of rejection can hold us back from taking risks and expressing our true selves. Yet, when we embrace vulnerability and authenticity, we open the door to real acceptance—both from others and, perhaps more importantly, from ourselves.

In this chapter, we'll dive into the fear of rejection, exploring how it shapes our choices and limits our potential. By understanding and reframing this fear, we can learn to face it with courage, freeing ourselves to live more authentically.

The Roots of Rejection: Why We Fear Being Turned Away

The fear of rejection is deeply intertwined with our sense of belonging and self-worth. As social beings, we're wired to connect with others; belonging was once essential to our survival. Early humans depended on the support and protection of the group to survive, so being rejected was a real threat. While the stakes may no longer be life-or-death, our fear of rejection still triggers a primal response.

Rejection feels so painful because it attacks our sense of self. When someone dismisses or criticizes us, we may interpret it as a reflection of our worth or abilities. Rejection from someone we admire, a job we dream of, or even a creative project can make us question our value. This fear can become so overwhelming that we develop protective mechanisms to avoid any situation that could lead to rejection. We may play it safe, hide our authentic selves, or avoid taking risks altogether.

The Impact of Rejection on Authenticity and Vulnerability

Ironically, the fear of rejection often prevents us from showing up authentically. We believe that if we present only the "acceptable" parts of ourselves, we'll have a better chance of being liked or valued. But this strategy only leads to shallow connections and limits our potential for growth. True acceptance and belonging come from being seen and accepted for who we genuinely are, not from presenting a curated version of ourselves.

When we avoid vulnerability, we lose the opportunity to experience true connection. By concealing our needs, dreams, and even flaws, we create distance between ourselves and others. While hiding behind a facade might seem protective, it prevents the very thing we're seeking: genuine acceptance and belonging.

Embracing Vulnerability: The Path to Real Acceptance

Vulnerability is the key to breaking free from the fear of rejection. When we allow ourselves to be vulnerable, we're choosing to show up as we are, without guarantees. Vulnerability means opening up about our fears, needs, and dreams, even if it feels uncomfortable or risky. In this openness, we invite others to see us more fully, creating space for true connection.

Embracing vulnerability doesn't mean putting ourselves in situations where we're certain to be hurt. Instead, it means stepping into life with a willingness to be seen for who we really are. The paradox of vulnerability is that, while it feels risky, it often leads to the most rewarding experiences of our lives. By showing up authentically, we give others the chance to connect with our true selves. Those who accept us in our vulnerability are the ones who will genuinely value and respect us.

Redefining Rejection: A New Perspective

One of the most empowering steps in overcoming the fear of rejection is to reframe what rejection means. Rejection often feels like a judgment against our worth, but in reality, it's usually a matter of compatibility or preference. Each person we encounter has their own set of beliefs, experiences, and needs. If someone chooses not to accept or connect with us, it often says more about them than it does about us.

Learning to see rejection as a part of life—rather than as a reflection of our value—can lessen its sting. With this mindset, rejection becomes less of a personal defeat and more of a redirection toward opportunities or people who are a better fit. Every time we face rejection, we gain valuable insights into who we are and what we want, and we're one step closer to the connections and experiences that truly align with us.

Building Resilience to Rejection: Practical Steps

Building resilience to rejection allows us to approach new situations with courage and openness. Here are some steps to help shift our perspective and strengthen our ability to face rejection:

Challenge Negative Self-Talk: After experiencing rejection, it's common to engage in negative self-talk, thinking things like "I'm not good enough" or "I'll never succeed." Challenge these thoughts by reminding yourself that rejection doesn't define your worth. Practice reframing your self-talk to be more constructive and compassionate. Instead of "I'm not good enough," try "This wasn't the right fit, but I'm proud of myself for trying."

Separate Yourself from the Outcome: Recognize that not every situation will result in acceptance, and that's okay. Whether it's applying for a job, asking someone out, or sharing your creative work, remind yourself that your value isn't tied to the outcome. Instead, focus on the courage it took to try.

Practice Exposure: Facing the fear of rejection becomes easier with practice. Start by taking small risks in areas where rejection feels less threatening. For example, try expressing a unique opinion in a group setting or sharing a personal interest with a friend. These small acts of vulnerability build confidence, making it easier to take bigger risks over time.

Reflect on Past Experiences of Rejection: Take a moment to think back to times when you experienced rejection. How did those experiences shape you, and what did you learn from them? Often, what seems painful in the moment reveals itself as a valuable lesson down the road. Reflecting on past rejections can help you see them as stepping stones rather than setbacks.

Seek Out Supportive Connections: Surround yourself with people who value you for who you are. Sharing your fears and dreams with supportive friends or family members can help counteract the sting of rejection. Knowing that you have a foundation of acceptance provides the confidence to be vulnerable in other areas of your life.

The Power of Self-Acceptance: Finding Belonging Within

Ultimately, facing the fear of rejection is about cultivating a deep sense of self-acceptance. When we accept ourselves, we become less dependent on external approval. We recognize that our worth isn't determined by others' opinions, and we feel freer to take risks, knowing that we'll be okay regardless of the outcome.

Self-acceptance gives us the courage to be authentic and vulnerable, even in the face of possible rejection. By choosing to show up fully, we not only give others the chance to see us as we are but also foster a more profound sense of belonging within ourselves. True belonging doesn't come from molding ourselves to fit others' expectations; it comes from honoring our own.

Reflection: Reframing Your Relationship with Rejection

As you reflect on this chapter, consider how the fear of rejection has influenced your choices and actions. Are there parts of yourself you've kept hidden out of fear of being turned away? What small steps can you take to practice vulnerability and self-acceptance in the face of this fear?

Take a moment to journal about a recent experience of rejection. Write down what happened, how it made you feel, and any insights you've gained from it. Reflect on what this experience taught you about yourself, and consider how you might approach a similar situation in the future.

With each act of vulnerability, you move closer to genuine connections and deeper self-acceptance. As we journey onward, remember that rejection is simply part of life's rhythm, guiding us to places, people, and opportunities that are right for us. In the next chapter, we'll explore the fear of failure, another common obstacle to personal growth, and how embracing failure can open doors to new possibilities and resilience.

7

TAKING A STEP INTO THE UNKNOWN

Life begins at the edge of our comfort zones, yet stepping into the unknown can feel overwhelming. Our comfort zones are safe, familiar, and predictable, shielding us from risk and potential discomfort. But they also limit our growth, keeping us from experiencing the full breadth of life. When we summon the courage to step into new and uncertain situations, we gain resilience, discover untapped abilities, and broaden our understanding of the world.

In this chapter, we'll explore why leaving the comfort zone is essential for personal growth and provide practical strategies for facing the anxiety that comes with venturing into the unknown. By learning to tolerate the discomfort of uncertainty, we unlock new dimensions of courage and self-discovery.

The Comfort Zone: A Double-Edged Sword

Our comfort zone isn't necessarily a bad place. It offers a sense of stability, helps us manage stress, and allows us to feel confident in our routine. However, it also confines us to what is familiar and known. When we stay within these boundaries, we miss out on new opportunities, experiences, and personal growth. We may not realize it, but constantly choosing the safe and known keeps us from learning who we might become if we dared to take risks.

Growth occurs when we challenge ourselves, even if it means stepping into situations that feel uncertain or intimidating. Outside our comfort zone lies the "growth zone," where we build new skills, gain fresh perspectives, and cultivate resilience. Moving into this space doesn't mean abandoning safety altogether; rather, it's about gradually expanding our boundaries, building the confidence to tackle bigger challenges along the way.

The Fear of the Unknown: Why We Resist New Experiences

Humans are wired to seek safety and predictability. Facing the unknown often triggers our "fight-or-flight" response, as the brain perceives uncertainty as a potential threat. Even if the risk is minimal, our instinct to avoid discomfort can prevent us from trying new things or taking healthy risks.

The fear of the unknown can also be tied to our desire for control. In uncertain situations, we don't always know what to expect, and we may fear failure, embarrassment, or disappointment. These concerns are natural, but allowing them to dictate our actions keeps us from experiencing the rewards that come with stepping out of our comfort zones.

The Rewards of Embracing Uncertainty

While uncertainty can be intimidating, it also brings incredible rewards. Each time we face an unfamiliar situation, we challenge our limitations and expand our capabilities. We build confidence by proving to ourselves that we can handle discomfort and adapt to new environments.

Stepping into the unknown also fosters creativity and resilience. When we navigate uncertainty, we're often required to think on our feet and approach problems in new ways. Each new experience broadens our understanding and gives us fresh insights that enrich our lives. The more we embrace uncertainty, the more we develop a "growth mindset," seeing challenges as opportunities rather than obstacles.

Practical Strategies for Stepping Outside the Comfort Zone

Learning to handle the anxiety of new and uncertain situations takes practice. Here are some strategies to help you take steps into the unknown with greater confidence:

Start Small with "Micro-Risks": Begin by taking small, manageable steps outside your comfort zone. These "micro-risks" might involve trying a new hobby, meeting a new person, or speaking up in a group setting. By gradually increasing the level of challenge, you build confidence over time. Each small success reinforces the idea that you're capable of handling new situations.

Visualize Success: Visualization is a powerful tool for reducing anxiety. Before stepping into an unfamiliar situation, take a moment to imagine a positive outcome. Picture yourself feeling calm, capable, and successful. This technique helps rewire your mind to anticipate success rather than focusing on potential fears.

Reframe Fear as Excitement: The physical sensations of fear and excitement—racing heart, shallow breathing, nervous energy—are surprisingly similar. When you feel the anxiety of facing the unknown, try reframing it as excitement. Tell yourself, "I'm excited about this opportunity," rather than, "I'm afraid." This simple shift in mindset helps you approach new experiences with curiosity rather than dread.

Practice Mindfulness to Stay Grounded: Stepping into the unknown often causes our minds to race with "what ifs." Practicing mindfulness can help you stay present and avoid becoming overwhelmed. Focus on your breath, and bring your attention back to the current moment whenever anxious thoughts arise. By staying grounded, you reduce the mental burden of worrying about every possible outcome.

Set Small Goals and Celebrate Progress: Rather than aiming to transform your life overnight, set small, achievable goals for stepping outside your comfort zone. Each time you accomplish one, take a moment to celebrate it. Recognizing your progress builds momentum and reinforces the belief that you're capable of handling the unknown.

Seek Support and Accountability: Facing uncertainty can feel less daunting with the support of friends, mentors, or loved ones. Share your goals with someone you trust, and ask for their encouragement. Knowing that you have a support system can help alleviate the fear of venturing out on your own.

Accept the Possibility of Discomfort: Part of embracing the unknown is accepting that discomfort is natural. Rather than resisting it, acknowledge that it's a part of growth. Remind yourself that discomfort is temporary and that each experience will bring you closer to a life of greater freedom and fulfillment.

Reframing Setbacks as Learning Opportunities

Sometimes, stepping into the unknown doesn't go as planned. We may encounter setbacks, challenges, or even failures. However, these experiences offer valuable lessons. Each time we face a challenge, we gain insights that help us grow stronger and more adaptable. By reframing setbacks as learning opportunities, we reduce the fear of taking future risks and become more resilient.

For example, if you take a risk at work and it doesn't go as expected, reflect on what you've learned rather than focusing on the outcome. What skills can you improve? How can you approach the situation differently next time? Every experience, successful or not, contributes to your growth and prepares you for future challenges.

The Role of Self-Compassion: Being Kind to Yourself Along the Journey

Stepping outside of your comfort zone takes courage, and it's essential to be kind to yourself along the way. Self-compassion involves treating yourself with the same understanding and patience you'd offer a friend. When you encounter setbacks or feel anxious, remind yourself that these feelings are normal. Give yourself credit for trying, and acknowledge your progress, even if it feels small.

Self-compassion also helps us recover more quickly from setbacks. Rather than criticizing ourselves for perceived failures, we can approach each experience with patience and kindness, viewing each step as part of a journey of personal growth.

Reflection: Expanding Your Comfort Zone One Step at a Time

As you reflect on this chapter, consider an area of your life where you'd like to step into the unknown. What small steps could you take to move closer to this goal? Write down one or two "micro-risks" that feel challenging but achievable, and set a plan for taking these steps in the coming days or weeks.

Imagine the possibilities that await as you venture beyond your current boundaries. What skills could you develop? What connections could you make? Picture yourself embracing these new experiences with curiosity and resilience, knowing that each step forward brings you closer to a richer and more fulfilling life.

8

FINDING STILLNESS AMIDST FEAR

Fear can feel all-consuming, often taking over our thoughts and emotions, leaving little room for clarity or peace. In moments of fear, our bodies may react with heightened anxiety, causing us to react impulsively or shut down altogether. Yet, amidst the chaos of fear, there lies a powerful tool for regaining control: mindfulness. By cultivating stillness in the face of fear, we can ground ourselves, respond with intention, and navigate our emotions more skillfully.

In this chapter, we will explore mindfulness techniques designed to help you pause, center yourself, and find calm amidst fear. These practices will not only assist in managing anxiety but will also foster resilience and a deeper connection to the present moment.

Understanding Mindfulness: The Art of Being Present

Mindfulness is the practice of focusing your attention on the present moment without judgment. It invites you to observe your thoughts, feelings, and bodily sensations as they arise, creating a space for awareness rather than reactivity. In the context of fear, mindfulness allows you to recognize fear for what it is — a temporary emotional response — rather than allowing it to dictate your actions or overwhelm your senses.

When fear strikes, our natural instinct is to resist it or escape it, often leading to a cycle of anxiety and avoidance. Mindfulness encourages us to lean into the experience, acknowledging our fear without trying to fight it. This approach transforms fear from an adversary into an opportunity for growth and understanding.

The Science of Mindfulness and Its Impact on Fear

Research has shown that mindfulness can significantly reduce feelings of anxiety and fear. By training our minds to focus on the present moment, we can lower the activity in the amygdala, the part of the brain responsible for the fight-or-flight response. Mindfulness practice also strengthens the prefrontal cortex, enhancing our ability to regulate emotions and make rational decisions.

When faced with fear, mindfulness helps us create a buffer between the initial emotional response and our subsequent actions. Instead of reacting impulsively, we can pause, observe, and choose how we want to respond. This practice is particularly valuable in situations where fear threatens to cloud our judgment or escalate our anxiety.

Mindfulness Techniques for Finding Stillness

Here are several mindfulness techniques to help you cultivate stillness and calm in moments of fear:

Breath Awareness: One of the simplest and most effective mindfulness practices is focusing on your breath. When you notice fear creeping in, take a moment to pause and observe your breath. Inhale deeply through your nose, allowing your abdomen to expand, and then exhale slowly through your mouth. Repeat this for several cycles. By concentrating on your breath, you anchor yourself in the present moment and create space to observe your feelings without judgment.

Body Scan Meditation: This technique involves bringing awareness to different parts of your body, promoting relaxation and grounding. Find a comfortable position, either sitting or lying down. Close your eyes and take a few deep breaths. Begin by focusing on your toes, noticing any sensations or tension. Gradually move your attention up through your feet, legs, abdomen, chest, arms, neck, and head. Acknowledge any areas of discomfort, allowing them to soften with each exhale. This practice helps you reconnect with your body, offering a sense of safety amidst fear.

Grounding Techniques: Grounding techniques are designed to help you reconnect with the present moment and the physical world around you. Try the "5-4-3-2-1" technique: identify five things you can see, four things you can touch, three things you can hear, two things you can smell, and one thing you can taste. This practice engages your senses and shifts your focus away from fearful thoughts, drawing you back into the here and now.

Mindful Observation: Take a moment to observe your surroundings without judgment. Choose an object in your environment—a plant, a piece of art, or even a ray of sunlight filtering through a window. Allow yourself to notice the details: its color, texture, shape, and how it interacts with light. Engaging in mindful observation can help you step back from your fears and appreciate the beauty and wonder of the present moment.

Journaling: Writing down your thoughts and feelings can be a powerful mindfulness practice. When fear arises, take a few minutes to write about what you're experiencing. Describe your emotions, the thoughts running through your mind, and any physical sensations. This practice allows you to process your feelings and gain clarity on what you're afraid of, helping to externalize and diminish their power over you.

Mindful Movement: Engaging in physical activity with mindfulness can be an excellent way to release tension and find stillness. Whether through yoga, walking, or dancing, focus on the sensations in your body as you move. Notice how your muscles feel, the rhythm of your breath, and the connection between your body and the ground. Mindful movement invites presence and helps to ground you in your body, providing a release for built-up anxiety.

Create a Mindfulness Routine: Incorporate mindfulness practices into your daily routine to build resilience against fear. Set aside time each day, even if just for a few minutes, to practice mindfulness. Whether through meditation, deep breathing, or simply taking a mindful walk, establishing a routine creates a foundation of calm that you can draw on during moments of fear.

Cultivating Self-Compassion During Fearful Moments

While practicing mindfulness, it's important to cultivate self-compassion. Fear can evoke feelings of shame or inadequacy, leading us to judge ourselves harshly for feeling scared. Remind yourself that fear is a natural human experience; it doesn't make you weak or unworthy. Treat yourself with kindness, recognizing that you're doing the best you can in that moment.

When fear arises, practice saying supportive phrases to yourself, such as "It's okay to feel this way" or "I am allowed to take my time." By nurturing a compassionate inner voice, you create a safe space for yourself to process fear without added pressure or judgment.

Reframing Fear: Viewing It as a Teacher

As you develop mindfulness skills, you may find that fear shifts from being an adversary to a teacher. When you pause to observe your fear without judgment, you open the door to understanding its origins and the messages it carries. What is this fear trying to protect you from? What lessons can you glean from it?

Reframing fear in this way allows you to approach it with curiosity rather than avoidance. Instead of being consumed by anxiety, you can engage with fear, exploring it as a part of your journey toward self-discovery and growth. Each fearful moment becomes an opportunity to learn more about yourself and your needs.

Reflection: Integrating Mindfulness into Your Life

As you reflect on this chapter, consider how you can integrate mindfulness practices into your daily life. What techniques resonate with you? How can you create a space for stillness and observation during moments of fear?

Take a moment to journal about a recent experience where you felt fear. How did it manifest in your thoughts and body? What mindfulness technique could you have used in that moment to create stillness? Write down your thoughts and commit to practicing mindfulness the next time fear arises.

By cultivating stillness amidst fear, you learn to navigate your emotions with grace and intention. In the next chapter, we'll delve into the concept of failure, exploring how to embrace it as a vital component of growth and resilience. Together, we'll uncover the gifts hidden within our challenges and learn to redefine our relationship with setbacks.

9
THE ART OF SELF-COMPASSION

In our journey through fear, one of the most powerful tools we can cultivate is self-compassion. Often, we are our own harshest critics, especially when we confront our fears or encounter setbacks. We may berate ourselves for not being brave enough or for failing to meet our own expectations. However, practicing self-compassion can transform how we respond to our fears and failures, fostering a nurturing environment for growth and resilience.

In this chapter, we will explore what self-compassion is, why it matters, and how to cultivate it in our daily lives, particularly when facing the challenges that fear brings.

Understanding Self-Compassion: More Than Just Kindness

Self-compassion is not merely being nice to oneself; it encompasses three key components:

Self-Kindness: This involves treating ourselves with care and understanding rather than judgment. When we face difficulties or make mistakes, self-kindness encourages us to respond with warmth and support, just as we would for a dear friend.

Common Humanity: Recognizing that suffering and imperfection are part of the shared human experience helps to alleviate feelings of isolation. Understanding that everyone struggles with fear and failure fosters a sense of connection and compassion towards ourselves.

Mindfulness: Mindfulness allows us to observe our thoughts and emotions without becoming overwhelmed by them. It helps us acknowledge our fears and struggles while maintaining a balanced perspective, preventing us from spiraling into self-pity or excessive negativity.

Together, these components create a foundation for self-compassion, enabling us to face our fears with a gentler and more supportive attitude.

The Importance of Self-Compassion in Facing Fear

Self-compassion is particularly vital when navigating fear for several reasons:

Reduces Anxiety: When we practice self-compassion, we lower our stress and anxiety levels. By acknowledging our feelings without judgment, we create a safe space for our emotions, reducing their intensity and allowing us to approach them with clarity.

Promotes Resilience: Self-compassion enhances our ability to bounce back from setbacks. When we view failures and fears through a lens of kindness, we're more likely to learn from our experiences rather than dwell on them, fostering resilience.

Encourages Growth: A compassionate mindset encourages a growth-oriented perspective. When we make mistakes, instead of seeing ourselves as failures, we learn to view these moments as opportunities for growth and learning.

Strengthens Motivation: Contrary to popular belief, self-compassion does not lead to complacency. When we treat ourselves kindly, we are more motivated to improve and take risks.

Self-compassion fosters a sense of safety that allows us to step outside our comfort zones with courage.

Practicing Self-Compassion: Techniques and Exercises

Incorporating self-compassion into your life requires intentional practice. Here are several techniques to help you cultivate self-compassion, especially in moments of fear:

Self-Compassion Break: When you're feeling overwhelmed by fear or self-criticism, take a moment to pause and practice a self-compassion break. Close your eyes, take a few deep breaths, and remind yourself of the three components of self-compassion: self-kindness, common humanity, and mindfulness. Say to yourself: "This is a moment of suffering. Suffering is a part of life. May I be kind to myself in this moment."

Write a Compassionate Letter to Yourself: When you're struggling with fear, write a letter to yourself from the perspective of a compassionate friend. Address your fears and challenges, and offer words of kindness, support, and understanding. This exercise can help you reframe negative self-talk and foster a nurturing inner dialogue.

Practice Affirmations: Create a list of affirmations that promote self-compassion. Repeat these affirmations regularly, especially when fear arises. Examples include: "I am doing my best," "It's okay to feel afraid," and "I am worthy of love and kindness." Affirmations can help shift your mindset and reinforce self-compassion.

Visualize Self-Compassion: When faced with fear, visualize yourself surrounded by a warm, loving light. Imagine this light enveloping you and providing comfort, safety, and understanding. This visualization can help ground you in moments of fear and remind you to treat yourself with kindness.

Mindfulness Meditation: Incorporate self-compassion into your mindfulness practice. During your meditation, focus on your breath and acknowledge any fears or negative thoughts that arise. Instead of resisting these feelings, practice self-compassion by gently guiding your thoughts back to kindness and acceptance. Acknowledge the fear without judgment, allowing it to exist in a space of compassion.

Celebrate Small Wins: Acknowledge and celebrate your progress, no matter how small. When you confront a fear, take a moment to recognize your bravery and the steps you've taken. This practice reinforces self-compassion and motivates you to continue moving forward.

Navigating Fear with Self-Compassion: Real-Life Applications

To illustrate the power of self-compassion, consider the following scenarios in which it can be applied:

Fear of Public Speaking: If you're afraid of speaking in front of a group, remind yourself that many people share this fear. Acknowledge the discomfort you feel and treat yourself kindly, recognizing that it's okay to struggle. Instead of berating yourself for feeling anxious, offer words of encouragement: "I am capable, and it's normal to feel nervous."

Facing Rejection: If you experience rejection, whether in a personal or professional context, practice self-compassion by acknowledging your feelings of hurt and disappointment. Instead of internalizing the rejection, remind yourself that everyone experiences setbacks. Treat yourself with kindness and allow yourself to grieve, knowing that this experience does not define your worth.

Taking Risks: When you decide to take a leap into the unknown, fear may arise. Instead of being critical of yourself for feeling anxious, practice self-kindness. Remind yourself of the courage it takes to step outside your comfort zone and celebrate your willingness to grow, regardless of the outcome.

Embracing Imperfection: The Path to Growth

Self-compassion is intimately tied to embracing our imperfections. In a world that often glorifies success and perfection, it can be challenging to accept our flaws and failures. However, acknowledging our humanity allows us to move forward with grace.

Instead of striving for perfection, aim for progress. Embrace the idea that mistakes are part of the journey and provide valuable lessons. When you encounter obstacles, remind yourself that growth often arises from discomfort and that every step, no matter how imperfect, contributes to your evolution.

Reflection: Cultivating Self-Compassion in Your Life

As you reflect on this chapter, consider how self-compassion can transform your relationship with fear. Write down instances where you've been hard on yourself in the past. How could self-compassion have changed your perspective? What practices will you implement to cultivate a more compassionate relationship with yourself?

Challenge yourself to embrace self-compassion as you face fears in the days ahead. Treat yourself as you would a dear friend: with love, understanding, and support.

10
BUILDING COURAGE ONE SMALL STEP AT A TIME

Courage is often perceived as a grand, dramatic act—the firefighter charging into a burning building, the activist standing up to injustice, or the athlete overcoming incredible odds to win. However, the truth is that courage is often found in the quiet, everyday moments of our lives. It is the small, incremental steps we take that build a foundation for greater bravery. This chapter emphasizes the value of these small acts of courage and how they can profoundly impact our journey through fear and personal growth.

Understanding Incremental Courage

Incremental courage is the idea that bravery doesn't have to be monumental; it can be cultivated through tiny, manageable actions. Just as a plant grows from a seedling to a towering tree, courage develops over time. Each small act of bravery nurtures our capacity to face more significant challenges, creating a ripple effect that enhances our resilience.

Consider the following:

Taking the First Step: The first step in any journey is often the hardest. It's easy to feel overwhelmed by the magnitude of a goal or fear, but breaking it down into smaller, actionable steps makes it more manageable. Each small step reinforces our belief in our abilities and fortifies our courage.

Building a Supportive Environment: Small acts of courage can also be nurtured in a supportive environment. Surrounding ourselves with people who encourage bravery allows us to take risks without fear of judgment. This community becomes a safety net, empowering us to step outside our comfort zones.

Celebrating Progress: Each small victory deserves recognition. Celebrating these moments boosts our confidence and serves as a reminder that we are capable of growth and change. This recognition reinforces the idea that every step, no matter how small, contributes to our journey.

Examples of Incremental Courage

To illustrate the concept of incremental courage, let's explore some real-life scenarios where small acts of bravery make a significant difference:

Speaking Up in a Meeting: For many, voicing opinions in a group setting can be intimidating. Instead of waiting for the perfect moment to share a groundbreaking idea, start by contributing small comments or asking questions. Gradually, these small contributions build your confidence, making it easier to share more significant insights in the future.

Initiating a Conversation: If you struggle with social anxiety, initiating conversations can feel daunting. Start with simple greetings or compliments to strangers. Each small interaction helps desensitize you to the fear of social engagement, eventually leading to deeper conversations and connections.

Trying Something New: Whether it's a new hobby, sport, or activity, the thought of trying something unfamiliar can evoke fear. Instead of diving into a challenging class or competition, begin with an introductory session or a casual gathering. Each new experience adds to your repertoire of skills and fosters courage to take on bigger challenges.

Setting Boundaries: Establishing boundaries is essential for maintaining healthy relationships but can feel uncomfortable. Begin with small, assertive statements, such as declining an invitation or expressing your needs. Each time you practice setting boundaries, you strengthen your ability to advocate for yourself.

Seeking Help: Many people struggle with the fear of seeking help, whether from a friend, therapist, or support group. Start by confiding in someone you trust about your feelings or challenges. Each time you open up, you take a courageous step towards healing and connection.

Practical Strategies for Building Incremental Courage

To cultivate incremental courage, consider the following practical strategies:

Set Small Goals: Break down larger goals into smaller, achievable tasks. For example, if your goal is to become a public speaker, start by practicing in front of a mirror or recording yourself. Gradually progress to sharing your message with a friend or a small group.

Create a Courage Journal: Maintain a journal dedicated to your acts of courage. Write down each small step you take, how it made you feel, and the impact it had on your journey. Reflecting on your progress reinforces the importance of incremental courage.

Practice Gratitude: Cultivate gratitude for the small acts of bravery you accomplish daily. Acknowledge the effort it takes to face your fears, no matter how minor the action may seem. Gratitude helps shift your focus from fear to appreciation for your growth.

Visualize Success: Spend time visualizing yourself successfully navigating fearful situations. Picture yourself taking small steps with confidence and courage. Visualization prepares your mind for real-life challenges and reinforces your belief in your abilities.

Join a Support Group: Surround yourself with like-minded individuals who are also working on their courage. Sharing experiences and encouraging one another creates a safe space for incremental bravery to flourish.

Overcoming Setbacks: Embracing the Learning Process

As we build courage, it's essential to recognize that setbacks are a natural part of the process. Not every attempt will go as planned, and that's okay. Rather than viewing setbacks as failures, embrace them as opportunities to learn and grow. Each stumble teaches us valuable lessons about ourselves and our capacities.

When faced with setbacks, practice self-compassion. Acknowledge your feelings of disappointment, but also remind yourself of the courage it took to try in the first place. Reflect on what you can learn from the experience and how it can inform your next steps.

Reflection: Your Journey of Incremental Courage

As you reflect on this chapter, consider the small acts of courage you can take in your life. What fears have you been avoiding? How can you break them down into manageable steps? Write down three small acts of courage you commit to taking in the coming week, and reflect on how each step contributes to your journey of growth.

Incremental courage is about embracing the journey rather than focusing solely on the destination. Each small step is a building block that strengthens your capacity to face greater challenges. In the next chapter, we will explore the power of vulnerability and how embracing our authentic selves can lead to deeper connections and a more fulfilling life. Together, we will learn that vulnerability is not a weakness but a profound strength that opens the door to true connection.

PART 2: CULTIVATING CURIOSITY (CHAPTERS 11-20)

11

THE SPARK OF CURIOSITY

Fear and curiosity often stand at opposite ends of the emotional spectrum, yet they share a profound connection. While fear can paralyze us, curiosity has the power to liberate, transforming our perceptions and inviting us to explore the unknown. This chapter introduces the shift from fear to curiosity, illustrating how cultivating curiosity can turn our fears into opportunities for growth and discovery.

Understanding the Power of Curiosity

Curiosity is an innate trait that drives us to explore, learn, and grow. It fuels our desire to ask questions, seek answers, and understand the world around us. When we approach life with curiosity, we become explorers in our own right, eager to uncover new experiences and insights. Here are a few ways curiosity serves as a catalyst for transformation:

Shifts Perspective: Curiosity encourages us to see the world through a different lens. Instead of viewing situations as threats, we can reframe them as opportunities for learning and exploration. This shift in perspective can diminish the hold of fear, allowing us to engage with our experiences more openly.

Fosters Resilience: A curious mindset nurtures resilience by promoting adaptability. When we encounter challenges, curiosity drives us to seek solutions and find creative ways to navigate obstacles. This resilience enables us to face fears with a sense of exploration rather than dread.

Encourages Growth: Curiosity propels us toward growth. It urges us to step outside our comfort zones, try new things, and learn from our experiences. This willingness to explore can lead to self-discovery and a deeper understanding of our strengths and passions.

Enhances Connection: Curiosity can deepen our relationships. By approaching others with genuine interest and curiosity, we create opportunities for meaningful connections. When we engage in open conversations, we foster understanding, empathy, and connection.

From Fear to Curiosity: A Transformative Journey

The transition from fear to curiosity is a journey that begins with awareness. Recognizing the fears that hold us back allows us to approach them with a curious mindset. Here's how to initiate this transformative shift:

Identify Your Fears: Take time to reflect on the fears that limit your experiences. Write them down and consider how they impact your life. By acknowledging these fears, you create a foundation for curiosity to take root.

Ask Questions: Transform your fears into questions. Instead of thinking, "What if I fail?" consider asking, "What can I learn from this experience?" Shifting your focus from fear to inquiry encourages exploration and a desire for understanding.

Embrace the Unknown: Curiosity thrives in the unknown. Instead of fearing uncertainty, approach it with an open mind. Embrace the idea that not knowing can lead to new discoveries and insights. This willingness to explore the unfamiliar fosters a sense of adventure.

Practice Mindfulness: Mindfulness allows us to stay present and observe our thoughts without judgment. When fear arises, practice mindfulness by acknowledging the feeling and then redirecting your focus toward curiosity. Ask yourself what aspects of the situation intrigue you or what you might discover by engaging with it.

Cultivate a Growth Mindset: A growth mindset—believing that abilities and intelligence can be developed—aligns perfectly with curiosity. Embrace challenges as opportunities for growth and learning. This mindset empowers you to view failures not as roadblocks but as stepping stones on your journey.

Real-Life Examples of Curiosity Transforming Fear

To illustrate the power of curiosity in transforming fear, let's explore some relatable scenarios:

Public Speaking: Many people fear public speaking due to the anxiety of judgment or failure. By shifting from fear to curiosity, you might ask yourself, "What makes a great speaker?" or "What can I learn from observing others?" This inquiry transforms the experience from one of dread to one of exploration, allowing you to discover your unique voice and style.

Traveling Alone: The idea of traveling alone can evoke fear of loneliness or danger. However, curiosity can turn this fear into excitement. Instead of focusing on what could go wrong, ask, "What incredible experiences might I discover?" or "What new cultures and perspectives can I encounter?" This shift opens doors to adventure and personal growth.

Starting a New Job: Entering a new work environment can be intimidating. Rather than fixating on potential challenges or fears of inadequacy, approach the situation with curiosity. Ask, "What can I learn from my new colleagues?" or "How can I contribute to this team?" This perspective invites a sense of exploration and connection.

Engaging in Difficult Conversations: Conversations about sensitive topics can trigger fear of conflict or misunderstanding. Instead of avoiding these discussions, cultivate curiosity about the other person's perspective. Ask questions and express genuine interest in understanding their point of view. This approach fosters deeper connections and mutual understanding.

Nurturing Curiosity in Daily Life

Curiosity is a skill that can be nurtured through practice. Here are several strategies to help you cultivate curiosity in your everyday life:

Ask Open-Ended Questions: Engage others by asking open-ended questions that invite exploration. Instead of yes-or-no questions, ask "What do you think about…?" or "How did that make you feel?" This fosters meaningful conversations and encourages curiosity.

Engage in New Experiences: Step out of your comfort zone and try new activities, whether it's taking a cooking class, exploring a new hobby, or attending a cultural event. Each new experience opens up avenues for curiosity and learning.

Create a Curiosity Habit: Dedicate time each week to pursue a new interest or hobby. This could involve reading about a topic you know little about, exploring a new place, or engaging in a creative project. By prioritizing curiosity, you allow it to flourish in your life.

Limit the Noise: In our fast-paced world, distractions abound. Reduce screen time and create moments of stillness where curiosity can thrive. Allow yourself to ponder questions, observe your surroundings, or engage in creative thinking without interruptions.

Reflect on Experiences: After trying something new or engaging in an experience, take time to reflect on what you learned. What surprised you? What did you enjoy? This reflection reinforces the value of curiosity and encourages future exploration.

Embracing Wonder: A Key to Transformation

As we learn to shift from fear to curiosity, we also tap into the profound sense of wonder that accompanies exploration. Wonder inspires creativity, joy, and enthusiasm for life. It allows us to see the beauty in the mundane and find excitement in the unknown.

Embracing wonder can be as simple as marveling at the beauty of nature, appreciating art, or being present in everyday moments. By allowing ourselves to be curious about the world, we awaken our sense of wonder and ignite a passion for discovery.

Reflection: Cultivating Curiosity in Your Journey

As you reflect on this chapter, consider the fears that have held you back. How can you reframe these fears into questions that inspire curiosity? Write down three areas in your life where you can cultivate curiosity and explore new possibilities.

Remember, curiosity is a powerful ally on your journey through fear. It opens doors to new experiences and perspectives, allowing you to embrace life with an open heart and mind. In the next chapter, we will explore the transformative power of vulnerability and how it can lead us to deeper connections and authentic living. Together, we will learn that embracing vulnerability is an essential step toward a fulfilling life.

12

UNPACKING CHILDHOOD DREAMS

As children, we are often filled with boundless imagination and the courage to dream without limits. We envision ourselves as astronauts, artists, or adventurers, believing that anything is possible. These childhood dreams are more than mere fantasies; they shape our identities, inform our choices, and influence our paths in life. This chapter invites you to reflect on those early dreams, exploring how they have molded who you are today and whether they still resonate within you.

The Importance of Childhood Dreams

Childhood dreams represent our purest aspirations and deepest desires. They emerge from a place of innocence and wonder, free from the constraints of societal expectations and fear. Revisiting these dreams can be a powerful exercise in self-discovery. Here's why reflecting on your childhood dreams is important:

Understanding Identity: Our early aspirations often reflect core aspects of our identity. They reveal our passions, interests, and values. By revisiting these dreams, we can gain insights into who we truly are and what brings us joy.

Reconnecting with Authenticity: As we grow older, the pressures of life can lead us to abandon our childhood dreams in favor of practicality or conformity. Reflecting on these dreams allows us to reconnect with our authentic selves, reminding us of the values and interests that once inspired us.

Recognizing Potential: Childhood dreams hold the potential for growth and exploration. They remind us that we have the capacity to pursue our passions and create fulfilling lives. Embracing these dreams can reignite our sense of purpose and possibility.

Healing and Acceptance: Some childhood dreams may have gone unfulfilled, leading to feelings of regret or disappointment. Revisiting these dreams allows us to process these emotions, understand the reasons behind them, and cultivate acceptance for our unique journeys.

Reflecting on Your Childhood Dreams

To embark on this reflective journey, find a quiet space where you can think and write. Take your time to ponder the following prompts that can help you unpack your childhood dreams:

What Were Your Dreams?: Recall the dreams and aspirations you had as a child. What did you want to be when you grew up? What activities made you feel alive and excited? Write down as many dreams as you can remember, allowing yourself to be free and unfiltered.

What Inspired These Dreams?: Consider the sources of inspiration for your dreams. Were they influenced by family, friends, media, or personal experiences? Reflecting on these influences can help you understand the motivations behind your aspirations.

How Did You Feel About These Dreams?: Examine the emotions you associated with your childhood dreams. Did they fill you with joy and excitement, or were they accompanied by fear of failure? Understanding your emotional relationship with these dreams can reveal valuable insights.

What Dreams Have You Pursued?: Reflect on the childhood dreams you've pursued and those you may have abandoned. Which dreams did you actively chase, and how did that shape your life? Conversely, consider which dreams fell by the wayside and why.

Do These Dreams Still Resonate?: Take stock of your current feelings toward your childhood dreams. Do they still hold meaning for you? Are there elements of these dreams you'd like to reclaim or explore further? This reflection helps clarify your present desires and aspirations.

Finding Meaning in Unfulfilled Dreams

While some childhood dreams may remain unfulfilled, they can still hold power and significance. Here's how to find meaning in these dreams:

Reinterpret Your Dreams: Unfulfilled dreams can be reinterpreted as lessons rather than failures. Consider what you learned from pursuing these dreams or what they taught you about yourself. This shift in perspective allows you to appreciate the value of your experiences.

Identify Themes: Look for recurring themes in your childhood dreams. For example, if you dreamed of being an artist, a scientist, and a storyteller, these aspirations may indicate a desire for creativity and exploration. Identifying these themes can inform your current interests and passions.

Create New Possibilities: If your childhood dreams no longer align with your current values or circumstances, consider how they might inspire new possibilities. For instance, if you once dreamed of traveling the world, think about ways you can explore your local area or engage in cultural experiences closer to home.

Integrate Dreams into Your Life: Find ways to incorporate elements of your childhood dreams into your present life. If you wanted to be a musician, consider taking up an instrument or participating in community music events. This integration helps revive your passions and fosters a sense of fulfillment.

Share Your Dreams: Discuss your childhood dreams with others. Sharing your aspirations can deepen connections and inspire others to reflect on their dreams. You may find support and encouragement from those who resonate with your journey.

The Role of Playfulness in Dream Exploration

Embracing a sense of playfulness is essential when revisiting childhood dreams. Allow yourself to dream freely without the weight of adult responsibilities or limitations. Engage in creative activities that reignite your imagination—draw, write, dance, or simply explore new hobbies. This playful approach fosters curiosity and opens the door to new possibilities.

Playfulness also encourages experimentation. Be willing to try new things without the pressure of success or perfection. Embrace the process of discovery and allow your dreams to evolve as you learn and grow.

Reflection: Rediscovering Your Dreams

As you reflect on this chapter, take time to write down your thoughts and feelings regarding your childhood dreams. Consider the following questions:

1. What childhood dreams still resonate with you today, and why?
2. How can you incorporate elements of these dreams into your life now?
3. What new dreams or aspirations have emerged from revisiting your past?

By rediscovering your childhood dreams, you can reconnect with the wonder and excitement of possibility. Embrace the lessons they offer and allow them to inspire your current journey.

13

ASKING THE RIGHT QUESTIONS

Questions are the engines of exploration and understanding. They open doors to new perspectives, encourage introspection, and foster deeper connections with ourselves and others. In this chapter, we will delve into the power of questions, discovering how asking the right ones can lead to transformative insights, personal growth, and a greater understanding of our fears, dreams, and experiences.

The Nature of Questions

Questions come in various forms, and not all questions are created equal. Some inquiries can lead us toward clarity and self-discovery, while others can perpetuate confusion and self-doubt. Here's how different types of questions function:

Closed Questions: These typically elicit a simple "yes" or "no" response. While they can be useful for gathering specific information, they often limit deeper exploration. For example, asking, "Did you enjoy the book?" may provide a quick answer but doesn't invite further conversation.

Open-Ended Questions: These questions encourage expansive thinking and deeper reflection. They often begin with "what," "how," or "why," prompting a more detailed response. For instance, asking, "What did you find most impactful about the book?" invites exploration and encourages meaningful dialogue.

Reflective Questions: These inquiries encourage self-examination and introspection. They help us consider our thoughts, feelings, and motivations. A reflective question like, "What emotions surfaced during that experience, and why?" prompts deeper understanding and personal insight.

Challenging Questions: These push us to confront our assumptions and beliefs. They can be uncomfortable but are essential for growth. A question like, "What fears are holding me back from pursuing my dreams?" encourages honesty and self-reflection.

The Power of Constructive Questions

Asking the right questions can lead to transformative insights. Here are some ways constructive questions empower personal growth:

Clarity and Focus: Constructive questions help clarify our thoughts and feelings, allowing us to focus on what truly matters. When we articulate our inquiries clearly, we create a pathway toward understanding and resolution.

Self-Discovery: Thoughtful questions encourage introspection and self-discovery. They guide us to examine our motivations, desires, and values, helping us uncover deeper truths about ourselves.

Problem-Solving: When faced with challenges, asking constructive questions fosters creative problem-solving. Instead of becoming overwhelmed, we can break down issues into manageable components, generating potential solutions.

Empowerment: Questions empower us to take ownership of our journeys. By exploring our thoughts and feelings, we can identify areas for growth, set goals, and develop actionable steps toward positive change.

Crafting Constructive Questions

To harness the power of questioning in your life, consider the following strategies for crafting constructive questions:

Be Specific: Instead of vague inquiries, aim for specificity. Instead of asking, "How can I be happier?" consider, "What specific activities bring me joy, and how can I incorporate them into my daily routine?" This specificity allows for actionable insights.

Use "What" and "How": Begin your questions with "what" and "how" to encourage exploration and reflection. For instance, "What are my core values?" or "How can I overcome my fear of failure?" These prompts invite deeper inquiry and understanding.

Avoid Judgment: Frame your questions without judgment. Instead of asking, "Why am I so lazy?" try, "What obstacles are preventing me from taking action?" This shift promotes self-compassion and encourages constructive exploration.

Encourage Reflection: Craft questions that invite reflection. Instead of asking, "What do I want to achieve?" consider, "What legacy do I want to leave behind, and what steps can I take to align my actions with that vision?" This reflection fosters a sense of purpose.

Explore Different Perspectives: Challenge yourself to consider different viewpoints. Ask, "How might someone else perceive this situation?" or "What advice would I give a friend facing this challenge?" This perspective-taking can illuminate new insights.

Examples of Constructive Questions

To illustrate the power of constructive questioning, here are some examples across various areas of life:

Career Exploration:

What aspects of my job do I enjoy the most, and how can I seek more of those experiences?
How do my skills and passions align with my career goals, and what steps can I take to bridge any gaps?

Personal Growth:

What limiting beliefs am I holding onto, and how can I challenge them?
How can I create a daily practice that nurtures my mental and emotional well-being?

Relationships:

What qualities do I value most in my relationships, and how can I cultivate those in my interactions?
How can I communicate my needs more effectively with the people I care about?

Facing Fears:

What specific fears are holding me back from pursuing my dreams, and what small steps can I take to confront them?
How can I reframe my perspective on failure as a learning opportunity rather than a setback?

Dreams and Aspirations:

What childhood dreams have I set aside, and how can I reconnect with them in my current life?

What steps can I take to align my current goals with my passions and values?

Creating a Questioning Practice

To integrate constructive questioning into your daily life, consider establishing a questioning practice:

Daily Reflection: Set aside time each day to reflect on your thoughts and feelings. Write down one or two constructive questions and explore them through journaling or contemplation.

Weekly Review: Each week, review your goals and aspirations. Craft specific questions that address any challenges or uncertainties you face, and use these inquiries to guide your actions for the week ahead.

Questioning Circle: Engage with friends or family in a questioning circle. Take turns asking each other constructive questions, allowing for deeper conversations and insights. This shared practice fosters connection and exploration.

Mindfulness and Meditation: Incorporate questions into your mindfulness or meditation practice. Choose a question to ponder during your practice, allowing insights to surface naturally as you sit in stillness.

Seek Feedback: Ask for feedback from trusted friends or mentors. Invite them to pose constructive questions that challenge your thinking and encourage self-reflection.

The Impact of Asking the Right Questions

As you incorporate constructive questioning into your life, you may notice a profound impact on your personal growth and self-awareness. Questions can lead to breakthroughs in understanding, clarity in decision-making, and a deeper connection with your authentic self. They encourage us to confront our fears, pursue our dreams, and navigate the complexities of life with curiosity and courage.

Reflection: Your Journey of Inquiry

As you reflect on this chapter, consider the following questions:

1. What are the most pressing questions in your life right now?
2. How can you reframe any limiting beliefs or fears into constructive questions?
3. What practices can you adopt to integrate questioning into your daily routine?

By harnessing the power of questions, you embark on a journey of self-discovery that leads to meaningful insights and transformative growth. In the next chapter, we will explore the theme of vulnerability, learning how embracing our authentic selves can lead to deeper connections and a more fulfilling life. Together, we will uncover the strength that lies in vulnerability and how it enriches our experiences.

14

THE MAGIC OF LEARNING SOMETHING NEW

Learning is a lifelong journey that opens doors to new experiences, ignites our passions, and fosters personal growth. In this chapter, we will explore the magic of learning something new, emphasizing the joy it can bring and the transformative impact it can have on our lives. By stepping outside of our comfort zones and embracing new skills, hobbies, or interests, we can discover hidden talents, challenge our fears, and reconnect with the curiosity that fuels our dreams.

The Joy of Discovery

Learning something new can be a thrilling experience. Whether it's picking up a musical instrument, trying your hand at painting, or exploring a new language, the act of discovery can awaken a sense of wonder and excitement. Here's why the joy of learning is so powerful:

Stimulating Curiosity: Engaging in new activities reignites our natural curiosity. It encourages us to ask questions, seek knowledge, and explore the world with fresh eyes. This curiosity can lead to unexpected insights and deeper understanding.

Building Confidence: Trying something new often comes with a sense of accomplishment. Each small success, whether mastering a new chord on the guitar or completing a painting, boosts our confidence and reinforces our belief in our abilities.

Fostering Creativity: Learning new skills stimulates our creative thinking. It encourages us to approach challenges from different angles and find innovative solutions. This creativity can spill over into other areas of our lives, enriching our experiences.

Creating Connections: New learning opportunities often provide avenues for connection with others. Whether through classes, workshops, or clubs, engaging with like-minded individuals fosters a sense of community and belonging.

Enhancing Adaptability: Embracing new challenges cultivates adaptability. It helps us become more comfortable with uncertainty and change, preparing us to face life's challenges with resilience and resourcefulness.

Identifying Opportunities for Learning

To embrace the magic of learning, it's essential to identify areas of interest that excite you. Consider the following ways to discover new learning opportunities:

Reflect on Interests: Take a moment to reflect on your interests and passions. What have you always wanted to try but never had the chance? What hobbies or skills have piqued your curiosity over the years?

Explore New Topics: Dive into areas of knowledge you know little about. Whether it's history, science, art, or technology, exploring new subjects can reveal hidden passions and interests.

Participate in Classes or Workshops: Seek out local classes or workshops in your community or online. Many organizations offer courses in various subjects, from cooking and gardening to coding and photography.

Engage with Online Learning Platforms: Take advantage of the wealth of knowledge available online. Platforms like Coursera,

Udemy, and Skillshare offer courses on a wide range of topics, allowing you to learn at your own pace.

Join Clubs or Groups: Look for clubs or groups that align with your interests. Whether it's a book club, hiking group, or craft circle, joining others in a shared activity provides motivation and inspiration.

Embracing the Learning Process

When embarking on the journey of learning something new, it's essential to approach the process with an open mind and a positive attitude. Here are some tips to help you embrace the learning experience:

Let Go of Perfection: Release the need for perfection. Learning is a process filled with mistakes and challenges. Embrace these moments as opportunities for growth rather than setbacks.

Cultivate Patience: Allow yourself the time to develop new skills. Progress may be slow at times, but patience is key. Celebrate small victories along the way, and recognize that mastery takes time.

Stay Curious: Approach your learning with curiosity and wonder. Ask questions, experiment, and explore different techniques. Let your imagination guide you as you delve into your chosen skill or hobby.

Create a Routine: Establish a regular practice routine that incorporates your new learning. Consistency can help solidify your skills and keep you motivated as you progress.

Seek Feedback: Don't hesitate to seek feedback from others, whether it's from a teacher, mentor, or peers. Constructive feedback can provide valuable insights and help you refine your skills.

Overcoming Fears Associated with Learning

While the prospect of learning something new can be exhilarating, it may also trigger fears or insecurities. It's common to feel apprehensive about trying new things, especially if we fear failure or judgment. Here's how to overcome these fears:

Acknowledge Your Fears: Recognize and accept any fears you may have about learning. By acknowledging these feelings, you can begin to address them and move forward.

Reframe Failure: Shift your perspective on failure. Instead of viewing it as a negative outcome, see it as a valuable part of the learning process. Each mistake is a stepping stone toward growth and improvement.

Visualize Success: Use visualization techniques to imagine yourself successfully engaging in your new skill or hobby. Visualizing success can help reduce anxiety and build confidence.

Start Small: Begin with small, manageable goals. This approach allows you to ease into the learning process without feeling overwhelmed. As you gain confidence, you can gradually tackle more significant challenges.

Celebrate Your Efforts: Acknowledge your efforts and progress, regardless of the outcome. Celebrate the courage it takes to step outside your comfort zone and embrace new learning experiences.

Reflection: Your Learning Journey

As you reflect on this chapter, consider the following prompts:

1. What new skills or hobbies have you always wanted to explore?
2. How can you incorporate learning into your daily routine?
3. What fears might be holding you back from trying something new, and how can you address them?

Embracing the magic of learning something new can ignite a passion for exploration and self-discovery. By stepping outside your comfort zone and allowing yourself to grow, you open the door to endless possibilities and enrich your life in ways you never imagined.

15
CURIOSITY ABOUT OTHERS

Curiosity is a powerful tool that can expand our understanding of the world and the people in it. In this chapter, we will explore how cultivating curiosity about others' experiences can enhance our empathy and foster deeper connections. By engaging with different perspectives and stories, we can enrich our own lives and contribute to a more compassionate and understanding society.

The Importance of Empathy

Empathy is the ability to understand and share the feelings of others. It allows us to connect with people on a deeper level and appreciate the diverse experiences that shape their lives. When we cultivate curiosity about others, we nurture our capacity for empathy, which has several important benefits:

Strengthening Relationships: Empathy enhances our relationships by fostering trust and emotional intimacy. When we take the time to understand others' perspectives, we create a safe space for open communication and connection.

Reducing Prejudice: Curiosity about others can help break down stereotypes and biases. By learning about different cultures, backgrounds, and experiences, we challenge our assumptions and cultivate a more inclusive worldview.

Enhancing Emotional Intelligence: Engaging with the experiences of others sharpens our emotional intelligence. It helps us recognize and respond to emotions, both in ourselves and in others, leading to more compassionate interactions.

Promoting Understanding: Curiosity encourages us to seek out diverse perspectives, which broadens our understanding of the human experience. This understanding fosters compassion and acceptance, even in the face of disagreement or conflict.

Engaging with Different Perspectives

To foster curiosity about others, it's essential to engage with different perspectives actively. Here are some strategies to help you do just that:

Listen Actively: When engaging in conversations, practice active listening. This means fully focusing on the speaker, withholding judgment, and demonstrating genuine interest in their experiences. Use open body language and maintain eye contact to show your engagement.

Ask Open-Ended Questions: Encourage deeper conversations by asking open-ended questions that invite others to share their stories. For example, instead of asking, "Did you like the event?" consider asking, "What did you find most meaningful about the event?" This approach opens the door to richer dialogue.

Seek Diverse Experiences: Expose yourself to diverse cultures, communities, and perspectives. Attend cultural festivals, read books from authors of different backgrounds, or engage in discussions with people whose experiences differ from your own. Each new encounter offers valuable insights.

Practice Perspective-Taking: Challenge yourself to put yourself in someone else's shoes. Consider how their background, experiences, and emotions influence their perspectives. This practice can help you develop a deeper understanding of their thoughts and feelings.

Share Your Own Stories: Curiosity is a two-way street. While it's essential to be curious about others, it's also valuable to share your own experiences. By being open about your story, you invite others to connect with you and foster mutual understanding.

The Power of Storytelling

Storytelling is a powerful medium for connecting with others and expanding our understanding of their experiences. Here's how you can harness the power of storytelling to enhance your curiosity:

Share Personal Stories: When you share your own stories, you create opportunities for others to connect with you on a deeper level. Consider moments in your life that have shaped your values and beliefs, and share these experiences with others.

Listen to Others' Stories: Make a conscious effort to listen to the stories of others. Everyone has a unique narrative that reflects their journey. By hearing these stories, you gain insights into their lives and the challenges they have faced.

Explore Different Mediums: Engage with stories through various mediums, such as books, podcasts, films, and documentaries. Seek out narratives that represent diverse voices and experiences, broadening your understanding of the human condition.

Create Safe Spaces for Sharing: Foster environments where people feel comfortable sharing their stories. This could be through organized storytelling events, community discussions, or informal gatherings with friends. Creating a supportive atmosphere encourages open dialogue and connection.

Reflect on the Stories You Encounter: After engaging with a story, take a moment to reflect on its impact. What emotions did it evoke? What new perspectives did it offer? Consider how these insights can shape your understanding of others and yourself.

Overcoming Barriers to Curiosity

While curiosity about others can be enriching, there may be barriers that prevent us from fully engaging with different perspectives. Here are some common barriers and strategies to overcome them:

Fear of Judgment: We may hesitate to ask questions or engage in conversations due to fear of judgment. Remind yourself that curiosity is a strength, and most people appreciate genuine interest in their experiences.

Assumptions and Stereotypes: Preconceived notions about others can hinder our curiosity. Challenge your assumptions by actively seeking out information that contradicts them. Approach each interaction with an open mind.

Cultural Differences: Engaging with people from different cultures can sometimes lead to misunderstandings. Embrace these moments as opportunities for learning. Be open to asking questions and clarifying meanings to promote understanding.

Time Constraints: Our busy lives may limit our opportunities to engage with others. Make a conscious effort to carve out time for meaningful conversations, whether through scheduled coffee chats, community events, or family gatherings.

Discomfort with Vulnerability: Curiosity often requires vulnerability, as it involves sharing and exploring personal experiences. Embrace this discomfort as a necessary step toward deeper connections and understanding.

Reflection: Expanding Your Curiosity

As you reflect on this chapter, consider the following questions:

1. What are some ways you can cultivate curiosity about the experiences of others in your daily life?
2. How can you actively engage with diverse perspectives and narratives?
3. What fears or barriers might be holding you back from exploring others' stories, and how can you address them?

Curiosity about others is a powerful catalyst for empathy and understanding. By embracing this curiosity, we can deepen our connections, challenge our assumptions, and contribute to a more compassionate world.

16

EMBRACING THE UNKNOWN WITH OPEN ARMS

Life is full of uncertainties and unexpected twists, and how we approach the unknown can significantly shape our experiences. In this chapter, we will explore how cultivating curiosity and openness toward the unknown can transform challenges into adventures. By shifting our perspective and embracing the unpredictable nature of life, we can foster resilience, creativity, and a sense of wonder that enriches our journey.

The Nature of the Unknown

The unknown can evoke a range of emotions, from excitement to fear. It represents the unexplored territories of our lives, filled with both potential and uncertainty. Understanding the nature of the unknown helps us approach it with curiosity rather than apprehension:

Source of Opportunity: The unknown is a wellspring of opportunity. Every challenge presents a chance for growth, learning, and self-discovery. By embracing the unknown, we open ourselves to new experiences that can shape our paths in unexpected ways.

Catalyst for Change: Change often arises from the unknown. It pushes us out of our comfort zones and compels us to adapt. While change can be daunting, it also encourages innovation and personal evolution.

Invitation to Explore: The unknown invites us to explore new possibilities. It encourages us to ask questions, seek answers, and uncover hidden potentials within ourselves and the world around us.

Shifting Perspective: From Obstacles to Adventures

When faced with the unknown, our mindset can significantly influence our response. Instead of viewing challenges as obstacles, we can reframe them as adventures. Here are some strategies to help shift your perspective:

Reframe Challenges: When confronted with uncertainty, consciously reframe your thoughts. Instead of thinking, "This is a problem," try reframing it as, "This is an opportunity for growth." This simple shift can change your emotional response to the situation.

Cultivate a Sense of Adventure: Approach life with a sense of adventure. View each challenge as a quest to uncover new insights about yourself and the world. Adopting an adventurous mindset can make even the most daunting tasks feel exciting.

Celebrate Uncertainty: Embrace the fact that life is inherently uncertain. Instead of resisting the unknown, celebrate it as a part of the journey. Recognize that the unpredictable nature of life often leads to the most meaningful experiences.

Visualize Positive Outcomes: Use visualization techniques to imagine positive outcomes from uncertain situations. Picture yourself navigating challenges with confidence and curiosity, discovering new strengths and insights along the way.

Stay Open to New Experiences: Maintain an open mind when faced with new opportunities. Be willing to try new things, meet new people, and explore different ideas. Openness can lead to unexpected connections and growth.

Curiosity as a Compass

Curiosity is an essential tool for navigating the unknown. It helps us approach challenges with an inquisitive mindset, turning obstacles into opportunities for exploration. Here's how to harness curiosity as your compass:

Ask Questions: Cultivate a habit of asking questions when confronted with uncertainty. What can I learn from this experience? How can I approach this challenge differently? Asking questions fosters a sense of wonder and exploration.

Embrace Experimentation: Allow yourself to experiment with new ideas and approaches. Failure is a natural part of experimentation, and it provides valuable lessons that contribute to personal growth. Be willing to take risks and learn from the outcomes.

Seek New Knowledge: When faced with the unknown, actively seek knowledge to inform your decisions. Research, read, and engage with others who have navigated similar situations. Expanding your understanding can empower you to approach challenges with confidence.

Practice Mindfulness: Mindfulness encourages us to stay present in the moment, reducing anxiety about the unknown. By practicing mindfulness, we can cultivate a sense of calm and clarity, allowing us to approach challenges with a clear mind and an open heart.

Reflect on Past Experiences: Reflect on past experiences where you embraced the unknown. Consider how those challenges ultimately led to growth or new opportunities. This reflection can serve as a reminder of your resilience and capacity to navigate uncertainty.

Transforming Fear into Curiosity

Fear is a natural response to the unknown, but it doesn't have to dictate our actions. By transforming fear into curiosity, we can approach challenges with a sense of wonder rather than apprehension. Here are some strategies to facilitate this transformation:

Acknowledge Your Fears: Recognize and accept any fears you may have regarding the unknown. By acknowledging these feelings, you can begin to address them and shift your focus toward curiosity.

Explore the Source of Your Fear: Delve into the root causes of your fear. What specifically makes you anxious about the unknown? Understanding the source can help you reframe your thoughts and focus on potential positive outcomes.

Find Inspiration: Seek inspiration from others who have embraced the unknown and turned challenges into opportunities. Read stories of individuals who took risks and discovered new passions or paths in life. Their experiences can motivate you to approach your own challenges with curiosity.

Create a Support System: Surround yourself with supportive individuals who encourage curiosity and exploration. Share your fears and challenges with trusted friends or mentors who can provide guidance and encouragement.

Practice Gratitude: Cultivating gratitude can shift your focus from fear to appreciation for the unknown. Reflect on the possibilities that lie ahead and the opportunities for growth. Gratitude fosters a positive mindset, helping you approach challenges with an open heart.

Reflection: Embracing the Unknown

As you reflect on this chapter, consider the following prompts:

1. What challenges are you currently facing that feel uncertain or daunting?
2. How can you shift your perspective to view these challenges as adventures?
3. In what ways can you cultivate curiosity about the unknown in your life?

Embracing the unknown with open arms can transform challenges into enriching experiences. By approaching uncertainty with curiosity and a sense of adventure, we unlock the potential for growth, creativity, and connection.

17

TURNING SETBACKS INTO STEPPING STONES

Life is an unpredictable journey, often marked by setbacks that can leave us feeling disheartened or defeated. However, the way we respond to these challenges can profoundly impact our growth and resilience. In this chapter, we will explore how curiosity can transform setbacks into stepping stones. By embracing failure as a teacher, we can uncover valuable lessons even in our most difficult moments.

The Nature of Setbacks

Setbacks are an inevitable part of life, whether they come in the form of personal failures, professional challenges, or unexpected obstacles. Understanding the nature of setbacks is crucial for developing resilience:

Universal Experience: Setbacks are a common experience for everyone, regardless of their background or achievements. Recognizing that you are not alone in facing difficulties can foster a sense of solidarity and reduce feelings of isolation.

Temporary States: It's important to remember that setbacks are typically temporary. While they may feel overwhelming in the moment, they often provide opportunities for growth and learning that can lead to future successes.

Catalysts for Change: Setbacks can serve as catalysts for change, prompting us to reassess our goals, strategies, and priorities. They encourage us to adapt and find new paths forward.

Opportunities for Self-Reflection: Facing setbacks allows us to engage in self-reflection, helping us understand our values, strengths, and areas for improvement. This introspection can lead to deeper self-awareness and personal growth.

Viewing Failure as a Teacher

Curiosity is a powerful tool that enables us to view failure as a teacher rather than a barrier. Here are some strategies for fostering this perspective:

Shift Your Mindset: When faced with a setback, consciously shift your mindset from one of defeat to one of curiosity. Ask yourself, "What can I learn from this experience?" or "How can this challenge help me grow?" This reframing can open your mind to new insights.

Identify Lessons Learned: After experiencing a setback, take time to reflect on the lessons it has taught you. Consider what went wrong, what could have been done differently, and how this experience can inform your future decisions. Document these lessons in a journal for reference.

Embrace a Growth Mindset: Cultivating a growth mindset involves believing that abilities and intelligence can be developed through effort and learning. This mindset encourages resilience and a willingness to embrace challenges as opportunities for growth.

Celebrate Small Wins: Even in the face of setbacks, it's essential to celebrate small victories along the way. Acknowledge your efforts and progress, no matter how minor. Celebrating these wins reinforces your resilience and motivates you to keep moving forward.

Practice Self-Compassion: Be kind to yourself in the face of failure. Instead of harshly criticizing yourself, practice self-compassion by acknowledging your feelings and treating yourself with the same kindness you would offer a friend. This nurturing approach fosters resilience and encourages a healthier response to setbacks.

Resilience: The Art of Bouncing Back

Resilience is the ability to bounce back from adversity and adapt to challenging circumstances. It's a skill that can be cultivated through curiosity and a willingness to learn from setbacks. Here's how to enhance your resilience:

Develop Problem-Solving Skills: When faced with a setback, focus on identifying solutions rather than dwelling on the problem. Engage in brainstorming sessions to generate ideas and explore alternative approaches.

Seek Support: Don't hesitate to reach out to friends, family, or mentors for support during difficult times. Sharing your challenges with others can provide new perspectives, encouragement, and valuable insights.

Stay Flexible: Embrace flexibility in your plans and expectations. Life is unpredictable, and the ability to adapt to changing circumstances is a hallmark of resilience. Cultivating a willingness to adjust your course can lead to unexpected opportunities.

Create a Resilience Toolkit: Assemble a toolkit of strategies and resources that can help you navigate setbacks. This may include techniques such as mindfulness, journaling, exercise, or creative outlets that provide comfort and clarity.

Reflect on Past Resilience: Recall instances in your life where you successfully overcame challenges. Reflecting on these experiences can remind you of your strength and resilience, providing motivation to tackle future setbacks.

Transforming Setbacks into Stepping Stones

When we approach setbacks with curiosity and an open mind, we can transform them into stepping stones on our journey. Here's how to do it:

Reframe Setbacks as Opportunities: Instead of viewing setbacks as failures, reframe them as opportunities for growth. Each challenge can serve as a stepping stone toward your goals, providing valuable insights along the way.

Set New Goals: Use the lessons learned from setbacks to set new, achievable goals. Break these goals down into smaller steps to create a clear roadmap for moving forward. This approach helps maintain momentum and focus.

Cultivate a Supportive Environment: Surround yourself with individuals who encourage resilience and curiosity. Engage with those who inspire you and provide constructive feedback, fostering an environment conducive to growth.

Embrace the Journey: Remember that personal growth is a journey, not a destination. Embrace the process of learning and evolving, and be open to the unexpected twists and turns along the way.

Share Your Experience: Consider sharing your setbacks and the lessons learned with others. By doing so, you not only reinforce your own understanding but also inspire others to embrace their challenges with curiosity and resilience.

Reflection: Learning from Setbacks

As you reflect on this chapter, consider the following questions:

1. What recent setbacks have you faced, and what lessons did they teach you?
2. How can you reframe future challenges as opportunities for growth?
3. What strategies can you implement to enhance your resilience in the face of adversity?

Turning setbacks into stepping stones requires a mindset of curiosity and a willingness to learn. By embracing failure as a teacher, we can transform our challenges into opportunities for growth and development.

18
CURIOSITY AS A PATH TO SELF-DISCOVERY

Curiosity is not just about seeking knowledge about the world around us; it is also a vital tool for understanding ourselves. In this chapter, we will explore how curiosity can lead to profound self-discovery. Through introspective exercises and reflective practices, you will uncover new layers of your identity, desires, and passions, enabling you to live a more authentic and fulfilling life.

The Role of Curiosity in Self-Discovery

Curiosity drives our quest for knowledge and understanding, and when applied to self-exploration, it can unlock new insights about who we are and what we truly desire. Here's how curiosity facilitates self-discovery:

Encourages Exploration: Curiosity invites us to explore the depths of our thoughts, feelings, and experiences. It encourages us to ask questions about our motivations, beliefs, and aspirations, leading to deeper insights about ourselves.

Fosters Openness: An attitude of curiosity fosters openness to new experiences and ideas. This openness allows us to challenge our assumptions, embrace change, and consider alternative perspectives about ourselves and our lives.

Promotes Reflection: Curiosity encourages us to reflect on our past experiences and how they have shaped us. By examining our histories with a curious mindset, we can gain a clearer understanding of our identities and the paths we wish to pursue.

Cultivates a Growth Mindset: Embracing curiosity nurtures a growth mindset, which promotes the belief that we can continually evolve and develop. This mindset allows us to approach self-discovery as an ongoing journey rather than a destination.

Introspective Exercises for Self-Reflection

To harness the power of curiosity in your journey of self-discovery, engage in the following introspective exercises:

The "Who Am I?" Reflection:

Set aside time in a quiet space with a journal. Write down the question, "Who am I?" and allow yourself to free-write without filtering your thoughts.
After a set period (e.g., 10-15 minutes), review your responses. Highlight or circle words and phrases that resonate most with you. This exercise can reveal aspects of your identity that you may not have considered before.
Life Timeline Exploration:

Create a timeline of your life, marking significant events, experiences, and turning points. Consider both positive and negative moments that have shaped your journey.
Reflect on how these events contributed to your current identity and desires. What patterns or themes emerge? What lessons can you draw from your past experiences?
Values Inventory:

Make a list of your core values—principles or beliefs that guide your decisions and actions. Use prompts such as "What do I stand for?" or "What matters most to me?" to help you identify your values.

Once you have your list, reflect on how these values align with your current life choices. Are there areas where you feel out of alignment, and how might you address this?

Exploration of Passions:

List activities that ignite your passion or bring you joy. Consider hobbies, interests, and pursuits that make you lose track of time or fill you with excitement.

For each activity, ask yourself what it reveals about your interests and desires. How can you incorporate more of these passions into your daily life?

Future Visioning:

Close your eyes and visualize your ideal life five or ten years from now. Where are you? What are you doing? Who are you with? Engage all your senses to create a vivid mental picture.

Afterward, write down your vision in detail. What steps can you take now to move toward this vision? This exercise can clarify your desires and aspirations.

Curiosity Journal:

Start a curiosity journal where you regularly jot down questions you have about yourself, your interests, or your experiences. Allow yourself to explore these questions through writing, drawing, or any creative medium.

Revisit your journal periodically, reflecting on how your questions and insights evolve over time. This practice encourages ongoing self-exploration and growth.

The Power of Curiosity in Challenging Assumptions

Curiosity enables us to challenge assumptions we may hold about ourselves. Here are some ways to leverage curiosity to question limiting beliefs and explore new possibilities:

Questioning Labels: Consider any labels you may have adopted about yourself (e.g., "I'm not creative" or "I'm not good at public speaking"). Approach these labels with curiosity: What evidence supports them? Are they truly accurate? Challenge yourself to explore experiences that contradict these labels.

Exploring "What If?" Scenarios: Engage in thought experiments by asking "What if?" questions related to your desires and identity. For example, "What if I pursued that dream I've always had?" or "What if I took a different career path?" This exercise can open up new avenues for exploration.

Seeking Feedback: Ask trusted friends or family members to share their perceptions of you. Approach this feedback with curiosity, seeking to understand how others view your strengths and potential. This external perspective can provide valuable insights that you may not have considered.

Embracing New Experiences: Step outside your comfort zone by trying new activities, meeting new people, or exploring unfamiliar interests. Each new experience offers an opportunity to learn more about yourself and what resonates with you.

Recognizing Growth: As you engage in self-discovery, recognize that your identity and desires may evolve over time. Embrace this growth with curiosity, allowing yourself the freedom to change and adapt as you learn more about who you are.

Reflection: The Journey of Self-Discovery

As you reflect on this chapter, consider the following prompts:

1. What aspects of your identity have you discovered through curiosity?
2. How have your desires evolved over time, and what have you learned from this process?

3. In what ways can you continue to cultivate curiosity as a means of self-discovery?

Curiosity is a powerful catalyst for self-discovery, allowing us to peel back the layers of our identities and desires. By engaging in introspective exercises and embracing an open mindset, we can uncover new truths about ourselves and live more authentically.

19

FUELING DREAMS WITH CURIOSITY

Dreaming big is a vital component of personal growth and fulfillment, yet many of us find ourselves stifled by fear, doubt, or societal expectations. In this chapter, we will explore how nurturing our dreams with genuine curiosity can help us expand our aspirations and make them more attainable. At the heart of this process lies self-belief—the unwavering faith in our potential to turn dreams into reality. By cultivating a curious mindset, we can explore new possibilities, embrace challenges, and fuel the passions that drive us forward.

Curiosity is the spark that ignites our aspirations. It invites us to ask questions, explore new ideas, and consider possibilities we might not have previously entertained. When we approach our dreams with curiosity, we open ourselves up to a world of exploration. Instead of viewing our ambitions as distant fantasies, we can begin to dissect them into smaller, actionable steps. This curiosity-driven approach allows us to uncover the 'why' behind our dreams, leading to a deeper understanding of what we truly desire and why it matters to us.

To dream big, we must first embrace the notion that our aspirations are valid and achievable. Self-belief is the cornerstone of this journey; it empowers us to pursue our dreams with confidence and resilience. When we believe in ourselves, we are more likely to take the risks necessary to reach for our goals. However, self-belief does not always come naturally; it is cultivated through experiences, reflections, and the support of others. By surrounding ourselves with positive influences and engaging in self-affirmation practices, we can strengthen our belief in our abilities and potential.

Nurturing our dreams also involves nurturing our curiosity about the paths we can take to achieve them. Instead of fixating solely on the end goal, we can explore the various avenues that may lead us there. This exploration might involve learning new skills, seeking mentorship, or even engaging in conversations with individuals who have pursued similar dreams. By asking questions and seeking guidance, we can gather insights and strategies that will help us navigate the complexities of our aspirations. Each new piece of information fuels our curiosity and encourages us to continue pushing forward.

Moreover, curiosity allows us to reframe setbacks and challenges as opportunities for growth rather than insurmountable obstacles. When faced with difficulties on our journey, we can ask ourselves what we can learn from the experience. This perspective shifts our focus from fear and frustration to exploration and adaptability. Embracing a curious mindset helps us remain resilient and open to change, ultimately strengthening our commitment to our dreams. We become more willing to experiment, iterate, and adapt our plans, all of which are essential components of success.

The connection between curiosity and creativity is also essential in fueling our dreams. Creativity thrives in an environment where questions are welcomed and exploration is encouraged. By allowing our imaginations to wander, we can generate innovative ideas and solutions that propel us toward our goals. Engaging in creative practices—whether through writing, art, or problem-solving—can deepen our understanding of our aspirations and lead us to new pathways. As we explore these creative outlets, we find that our dreams evolve, and new possibilities emerge.

Additionally, curiosity fosters a sense of wonder that can invigorate our aspirations. When we approach our dreams with a sense of excitement and eagerness to learn, we transform the pursuit of our goals into an enriching journey. This mindset encourages us to savor the process rather than fixating solely on the destination. Each step we take becomes a valuable lesson, filled with opportunities for growth and self-discovery. This perspective enhances our motivation and fuels our commitment to our dreams, making the journey as fulfilling as the achievement itself.

As we nurture our dreams with curiosity, we must also practice self-compassion. The journey toward our aspirations is often fraught with uncertainty and challenges, and it is crucial to treat ourselves kindly during difficult times. Recognizing that setbacks are a natural part of the process allows us to maintain our motivation and self-belief. By acknowledging our efforts and celebrating our progress, we reinforce our sense of purpose and strengthen our resolve. This compassionate approach fosters a healthy relationship with our dreams, allowing us to pursue them with both enthusiasm and grace.

In conclusion, dreaming big requires a foundation of self-belief, curiosity, and compassion. By nurturing our aspirations with genuine curiosity, we open ourselves to new possibilities and deepen our understanding of our desires. Embracing challenges and reframing setbacks as opportunities for growth will strengthen our resolve to pursue our dreams. As we fuel our aspirations with curiosity, we embark on a transformative journey of self-discovery, creativity, and resilience, ultimately leading us closer to realizing our most cherished dreams. In the next chapter, we will delve into the power of vulnerability, exploring how embracing our authentic selves can lead to deeper connections and personal growth. Together, we will learn to navigate the complexities of vulnerability and celebrate the strength it brings to our lives.

20
THE COURAGE TO QUESTION THE STATUS QUO

In a world that often prioritizes conformity over individuality, the courage to question the status quo is a vital catalyst for personal growth and self-discovery. Societal expectations and norms can impose rigid frameworks on how we define success, happiness, and fulfillment. In this chapter, we will explore the importance of critically examining these norms and assessing how our dreams align (or don't) with traditional paths. By embracing the courage to question established beliefs, we can carve out our own unique journeys and pursue the aspirations that resonate most with us.

At the heart of questioning the status quo lies a desire for authenticity. Many of us grow up internalizing societal messages about what it means to be successful—often reflected in conventional paths such as pursuing certain careers, obtaining specific degrees, or following established timelines for major life events. However, these expectations can lead us away from our true passions and desires. To foster authenticity, we must first become aware of the beliefs that have been ingrained in us. Reflecting on the origins of these beliefs and how they shape our decisions can illuminate whether they serve us or hinder our dreams.

To embark on this journey of questioning, we must cultivate a mindset of curiosity. Curiosity empowers us to ask probing questions about our choices, aspirations, and the influences that shape our lives. We can begin by examining the dreams we hold dear: Are they truly our own, or have they been influenced by external pressures? Are we pursuing them because they bring us joy, or because they align with what others expect of us? By engaging in this self-inquiry, we can discern which dreams resonate authentically and which may need reevaluation.

One effective exercise in this exploration is to create a personal values assessment. By identifying our core values, we can better understand how they align with our dreams and the societal norms we encounter. Consider what truly matters to you: Is it creativity, freedom, connection, innovation, or something else? Once you have identified your values, reflect on how they manifest in your life and aspirations. Are there areas where you feel out of alignment? This assessment can provide clarity on where your true passions lie and where societal expectations may be steering you off course.

Challenging the status quo also requires us to confront our fears and the discomfort that often accompanies stepping outside established norms. Fear of judgment, rejection, or failure can be paralyzing, preventing us from pursuing unconventional paths. However, it is essential to recognize that these fears often stem from the very societal expectations we seek to question. By reframing our perspective on fear as a natural part of growth, we can cultivate the courage to take risks and embrace the unknown. Acknowledging that discomfort is a sign of progress can empower us to venture beyond our comfort zones and pursue our authentic dreams.

As we navigate this journey of questioning societal norms, we can draw inspiration from those who have dared to challenge the status quo before us. History is replete with individuals who defied conventional paths to pursue their unique visions—artists, innovators, activists, and thinkers who reshaped the world through their courage. Their stories remind us that while questioning the status quo may be daunting, it can also lead to transformative change, both personally and collectively. By sharing these narratives, we can find motivation and strength in knowing that we are part of a larger movement toward authenticity and self-expression.

Moreover, it is crucial to engage in conversations about societal expectations with those around us. Sharing our thoughts and feelings about the pressures we face can create a supportive environment for questioning norms. By encouraging open dialogue, we can foster a sense of community that celebrates individuality and diverse aspirations. Engaging with others who share similar experiences can provide validation and encouragement, reminding us that we are not alone in our quest for authenticity.

As we question the status quo, we also have an opportunity to redefine what success means to us personally. Rather than adhering to traditional metrics of achievement, we can create our own definitions based on our values, passions, and dreams. This redefinition allows us to pursue fulfillment on our terms, aligning our goals with our authentic selves. As we craft our unique definitions of success, we empower ourselves to pursue paths that resonate deeply with our identities, regardless of how they compare to societal expectations.

In conclusion, questioning the status quo is a courageous act that invites us to explore our authentic selves and align our dreams with our values. By critically examining societal expectations and norms, we can discern which paths serve us and which need reevaluation. Embracing curiosity and engaging in self-inquiry enables us to uncover our true aspirations, while fostering a supportive community helps us navigate the challenges that arise when challenging established beliefs. As we embark on this journey of authenticity, we redefine success on our terms and pursue our dreams with courage and conviction. In the next chapter, we will delve into the profound theme of vulnerability, exploring how embracing our authentic selves can lead to deeper connections and personal growth. Together, we will learn to navigate the complexities of vulnerability and celebrate the strength it brings to our lives.

111 The Bravest Me: A Journey Through Fears and Dreams

PART 3: NURTURING COMPASSION (CHAPTERS 21-30)

21

THE POWER OF SELF-COMPASSION

As we continue our journey of self-discovery and personal growth, it's essential to circle back to one of the most transformative concepts we've explored: self-compassion. In this chapter, we will delve into the profound power of self-compassion and how it acts as a vital support system for healing and personal growth, particularly during times when courage falters. In a world that often champions resilience and strength, self-compassion invites us to embrace our vulnerabilities and treat ourselves with the same kindness we would offer a friend in times of struggle.

Self-compassion is more than just being kind to ourselves; it encompasses a deep understanding of our shared humanity. It recognizes that imperfection and suffering are part of the human experience, allowing us to acknowledge our struggles without judgment. When we practice self-compassion, we create a safe space for ourselves to experience our feelings fully, whether they are rooted in fear, disappointment, or failure. This acceptance is the first step toward healing, as it allows us to confront our emotional pain without the added burden of shame or self-criticism.

During moments of vulnerability or when courage wavers, self-compassion serves as a comforting anchor. Life can present us with challenges that shake our confidence and make us question our worth. In these moments, it is easy to fall into a cycle of negative self-talk and self-doubt. However, when we practice self-compassion, we can counteract these harsh inner narratives with understanding and empathy. Instead of berating ourselves for perceived shortcomings, we can acknowledge our feelings and remind ourselves that it is okay to struggle. This shift in perspective fosters resilience and enables us to navigate difficulties with a gentler heart.

Research has shown that self-compassion is linked to numerous positive outcomes, including greater emotional resilience, reduced anxiety, and increased motivation. When we approach ourselves with kindness, we create a supportive inner dialogue that encourages growth rather than fear of failure. This compassionate mindset fosters a sense of safety that allows us to take risks, try new things, and pursue our dreams without the paralyzing fear of judgment. Instead of seeing mistakes as reflections of our worth, we can view them as valuable learning experiences that contribute to our growth.

One practical way to cultivate self-compassion is through mindfulness. Mindfulness encourages us to be present with our thoughts and feelings without judgment. By developing this awareness, we can catch ourselves in moments of self-criticism and gently redirect our thoughts towards compassion. For instance, when you find yourself feeling inadequate, take a moment to breathe deeply and reflect on the reality of your situation. Remind yourself that it is human to feel this way and that many others experience similar struggles. By acknowledging this shared experience, you can cultivate a sense of connection and understanding with yourself.

Another powerful practice is the "self-compassion break." This exercise involves taking a few moments to pause when you are feeling overwhelmed or critical of yourself. Begin by recognizing your emotional pain and acknowledging that it is part of being human. Then, speak to yourself as you would to a dear friend, using words of encouragement and kindness. Finally, reflect on what you need in that moment—whether it's support, understanding, or a specific action. This practice helps reinforce the idea that you are deserving of compassion and care, no matter the circumstances.

Self-compassion also plays a critical role in the process of healing from past traumas and setbacks. When we face painful memories or unresolved issues, it is easy to become overwhelmed by feelings of shame or guilt. However, self-compassion allows us to approach these experiences with gentleness and understanding. Instead of avoiding or repressing our emotions, we can acknowledge them and create space for healing. By treating ourselves with compassion, we open the door to forgiveness and acceptance, which are essential for moving forward.

As we cultivate self-compassion, it is important to recognize that it is not a one-time achievement but an ongoing practice. Just as we invest time in nurturing our relationships with others, we must also prioritize our relationship with ourselves. This involves regularly checking in with our feelings, celebrating our achievements, and offering ourselves kindness during difficult times. As we integrate self-compassion into our daily lives, we strengthen our emotional resilience and create a solid foundation for personal growth.

The power of self-compassion is profound and transformative. It supports healing and personal growth, especially during moments when courage falters. By embracing our vulnerabilities and treating ourselves with kindness, we create a nurturing environment that fosters resilience and self-acceptance. As we practice self-compassion, we develop a compassionate inner voice that empowers us to navigate challenges, learn from our experiences, and pursue our dreams with renewed confidence. In the next chapter, we will explore the theme of vulnerability and how embracing our authentic selves can lead to deeper connections and personal growth. Together, we will learn to navigate the complexities of vulnerability and celebrate the strength it brings to our lives.

22
COMPASSIONATE CONNECTIONS

Compassion is a powerful force that extends beyond our relationship with ourselves; it profoundly influences our connections with others. In this chapter, we will explore the role of compassion in nurturing relationships and how cultivating compassionate connections can enhance our personal journeys. By understanding the importance of active listening, empathy, and care for others, we can create deeper, more meaningful interactions that not only support those around us but also foster our own growth and well-being.

At the heart of compassionate connections lies active listening. This practice involves being fully present and engaged during conversations, creating a safe space for others to express their thoughts and feelings. Active listening requires more than just hearing words; it demands our complete attention, open-mindedness, and genuine curiosity about the speaker's experience. By giving our full attention, we show others that their feelings and perspectives are valid and worthy of consideration. This practice nurtures trust and understanding, laying the foundation for a compassionate relationship.

Empathy is another vital component of compassionate connections. It allows us to put ourselves in another person's shoes and understand their emotions and experiences from their perspective. Empathy goes beyond sympathy, which often involves feeling sorry for someone; instead, it invites us to connect with the emotions that others are experiencing. When we practice empathy, we acknowledge the struggles and joys of others, creating an environment where they feel seen and understood. This shared emotional connection fosters a sense of belonging and reinforces our shared humanity.

Caring for others can be a transformative experience, enriching our lives in unexpected ways. When we extend compassion to those around us, we not only help them feel valued, but we also nurture our own emotional well-being. Engaging in acts of kindness, whether small or significant, cultivates a sense of purpose and fulfillment. Studies have shown that helping others can lead to increased happiness and reduced feelings of isolation. This reciprocal relationship between giving and receiving compassion highlights the interconnectedness of our experiences and the impact we have on one another's lives.

Compassionate connections also offer an opportunity for personal growth. When we engage in meaningful relationships, we learn valuable lessons about ourselves and the world around us. Through our interactions with others, we can gain new perspectives, challenge our assumptions, and develop a deeper understanding of different experiences. These lessons can lead to greater self-awareness and emotional intelligence, essential components of personal growth. By fostering connections rooted in compassion, we create a rich tapestry of experiences that contribute to our overall journey.

However, building compassionate connections requires vulnerability. It often involves sharing our own experiences and emotions, which can feel daunting. Yet, vulnerability is a strength that fosters deeper connections. When we allow ourselves to be open and authentic, we invite others to do the same. This reciprocal vulnerability creates a safe space for honesty and understanding, allowing compassion to flourish. Embracing vulnerability also empowers us to seek support when needed, reinforcing the idea that we do not have to navigate our journeys alone.

In addition to active listening and empathy, setting healthy boundaries is essential for nurturing compassionate connections. While it is important to care for others, we must also prioritize our own well-being. Compassionate relationships are built on mutual respect, and establishing boundaries ensures that we can maintain our energy and emotional health while supporting those we care about. By communicating our limits clearly, we model healthy relationship dynamics and create a space where both parties can thrive. This balance allows us to be present for others without sacrificing our own needs.

Cultivating compassionate connections also involves recognizing and celebrating the strengths and contributions of others. When we acknowledge the unique qualities that each person brings to our lives, we foster an atmosphere of appreciation and gratitude. Celebrating the achievements and milestones of those we care about reinforces the bonds we share and encourages a culture of support. By actively expressing our appreciation, we create a positive feedback loop that nurtures both our relationships and our individual journeys.

Finally, compassion extends beyond our immediate relationships; it has the potential to ripple out into the broader community. By embodying compassion in our interactions, we inspire others to do the same. Our small acts of kindness can create a chain reaction, fostering a culture of empathy and support that transcends individual connections. This collective compassion can contribute to a more caring and connected society, where everyone feels valued and supported in their journey.

Compassionate connections play a vital role in nurturing our relationships and enhancing our personal growth. Through active listening, empathy, and care for others, we create meaningful interactions that foster trust and understanding. As we engage in compassionate relationships, we not only support those around us but also enrich our own journeys. By embracing vulnerability and establishing healthy boundaries, we create an environment where compassion can thrive. Ultimately, our ability to connect with others compassionately enhances our shared humanity, reminding us that we are all on this journey together. In the next chapter, we will explore the importance of gratitude and how cultivating an attitude of appreciation can transform our perspectives and deepen our connections. Together, we will learn to recognize the beauty in our lives and the impact it has on our overall well-being.

23

THE STRENGTH IN VULNERABILITY

Vulnerability is often perceived as a weakness—a sentiment that discourages us from expressing our true selves and seeking deeper connections with others. However, in this chapter, we will explore vulnerability as a profound strength, examining how embracing our authentic selves fosters true connections and cultivates the courage needed to navigate life's challenges. Through stories and examples, we will uncover the transformative power of vulnerability and how it can lead to deeper relationships, personal growth, and a more fulfilling life.

To begin, let's redefine vulnerability. It is not merely about exposing our weaknesses or fears; rather, it is about being honest and open about our experiences, emotions, and desires. When we allow ourselves to be vulnerable, we invite others into our lives and create opportunities for genuine connection. This openness lays the groundwork for trust, as it demonstrates our willingness to share our authentic selves without the facade of perfection. As Brené Brown, a leading researcher on vulnerability, famously states, "Vulnerability is the birthplace of innovation, creativity, and change." By embracing vulnerability, we can unlock our true potential and create meaningful relationships.

Consider the story of a woman named Sarah, who found herself grappling with anxiety after a significant life change. For years, she hid her struggles, putting on a brave face for her friends and family. However, when she decided to share her feelings of fear and uncertainty with a close friend, she discovered that her vulnerability was met with understanding and support. This honest conversation not only deepened their friendship but also allowed Sarah to process her emotions in a safe space. By embracing her vulnerability, she transformed her experience from one of isolation to one of connection, highlighting the strength that comes from sharing our struggles with others.

The strength in vulnerability also extends to our ability to foster courage. When we confront our fears and allow ourselves to be seen authentically, we cultivate a sense of bravery that empowers us to face life's challenges head-on. Vulnerability encourages us to take risks—whether that means pursuing a passion, engaging in a difficult conversation, or expressing our true feelings. For instance, a man named David, who had long suppressed his passion for art due to societal expectations, found the courage to share his artwork at a local gallery after years of hesitation. By embracing his vulnerability and sharing his authentic self, David not only pursued his dreams but also inspired others to do the same. His story serves as a reminder that vulnerability can fuel our courage and lead to transformative experiences.

Additionally, vulnerability can foster true connections by allowing others to relate to our experiences. When we share our struggles, we create an opportunity for others to do the same. This reciprocal exchange deepens our relationships and reinforces the idea that we are not alone in our challenges. In a world where social media often presents curated versions of our lives, embracing vulnerability can help combat feelings of isolation and comparison. By sharing our authentic experiences, we cultivate a sense of belonging that resonates with others, reminding us of our shared humanity.

Moreover, vulnerability is a critical component of emotional intimacy in our relationships. When we allow ourselves to be vulnerable, we create an environment where honesty and openness can thrive. This emotional intimacy strengthens the bonds we share with others and fosters a deeper understanding of one another. For example, in a romantic relationship, being vulnerable about our fears, desires, and insecurities can deepen trust and create a solid foundation for lasting connection. Couples who embrace vulnerability often find that their relationship flourishes as they navigate challenges together with honesty and empathy.

While embracing vulnerability can be challenging, it is essential to acknowledge that vulnerability does not mean exposing ourselves to harm or allowing others to take advantage of our openness. Setting boundaries is crucial in maintaining healthy relationships while still allowing ourselves to be vulnerable. By practicing discernment in our interactions, we can create safe spaces for vulnerability without compromising our well-being. This balance allows us to share our authentic selves while protecting our emotional health.

To cultivate vulnerability in our lives, we can begin by embracing small acts of openness. This may involve sharing our thoughts and feelings with a trusted friend, expressing our needs in a relationship, or pursuing a passion that scares us. These incremental steps help build our resilience and create a habit of vulnerability, ultimately leading to more significant and profound connections. As we practice vulnerability, we may also inspire those around us to embrace their authentic selves, creating a ripple effect of openness and connection in our communities.

Vulnerability is a remarkable strength that allows us to foster true connections, cultivate courage, and embrace our authentic selves. By sharing our experiences and emotions honestly, we create opportunities for deeper relationships and personal growth. As we learn to embrace vulnerability, we unlock the power to connect with others in meaningful ways, transforming our relationships and enhancing our overall well-being. In the next chapter, we will explore the theme of gratitude and how cultivating an attitude of appreciation can further enrich our lives and strengthen our connections with others. Together, we will learn to recognize and celebrate the beauty in our lives, fostering a sense of fulfillment and joy.

24
FORGIVENESS AS A PATH TO FREEDOM

Forgiveness is a powerful and liberating practice that has the potential to transform our lives in profound ways. In this chapter, we will explore forgiveness not just as a means of letting go of grievances toward others, but as a vital practice of self-forgiveness. This journey toward forgiveness is a path to freedom, enabling us to release the burdens of past mistakes and emotional wounds that hold us back from living fully in the present. Through understanding the essence of forgiveness, we can unlock a new level of emotional well-being and personal growth.

At its core, forgiveness is an act of compassion—both toward others and ourselves. It does not condone harmful actions or minimize the pain caused by those actions; rather, it acknowledges the hurt while choosing to release its grip on our lives. Forgiveness allows us to reclaim our power and move forward, unshackled by the chains of resentment and anger. By practicing forgiveness, we cultivate a sense of peace that can profoundly affect our mental and emotional health, leading to improved relationships and a more positive outlook on life.

Self-forgiveness, in particular, is a critical aspect of this process. Many of us carry the weight of past mistakes, berating ourselves for choices we regret or actions we wish we could change. This internal dialogue often leads to feelings of shame and unworthiness, which can inhibit our ability to grow and thrive. However, self-forgiveness invites us to recognize our humanity and acknowledge that everyone makes mistakes. It encourages us to treat ourselves with the same kindness and understanding we would extend to a friend who is struggling. By embracing self-forgiveness, we can release the negative emotions tied to our past actions and make space for healing and growth.

Consider the story of Emily, who struggled with feelings of guilt after ending a long-term relationship. She believed that her decision had hurt her partner and often replayed moments of their time together, wishing she had acted differently. This pattern of self-blame weighed heavily on her, affecting her self-esteem and ability to move forward. It wasn't until she began to practice self-forgiveness that she started to heal. By recognizing that her decision was made with the best intentions for both herself and her partner, Emily was able to release the guilt that had been holding her captive. This shift not only allowed her to find peace but also opened her heart to new possibilities in her life.

The process of self-forgiveness often involves three key steps: acknowledgment, reflection, and compassion. The first step, acknowledgment, requires us to confront our past mistakes honestly. This may involve journaling or engaging in deep reflection to fully understand the impact of our actions on ourselves and others. By acknowledging the pain we've caused, we take the first step toward healing.

Next comes reflection, where we consider the lessons learned from our experiences. What insights can we take away from our mistakes? How can they inform our future choices? This step encourages us to shift our focus from blame to growth, recognizing that our missteps contribute to our overall journey. This reflective practice fosters self-awareness and helps us develop a more compassionate view of ourselves.

Finally, we must practice compassion toward ourselves. This involves treating ourselves with kindness and understanding as we navigate the complexities of forgiveness. It is essential to remind ourselves that we are worthy of love and acceptance, despite our imperfections. Engaging in positive self-talk and seeking support from loved ones can reinforce this compassionate mindset, allowing us to embrace our humanity fully.

It is important to note that forgiveness is not a linear process; it may involve setbacks and require ongoing effort. Just as we may need to forgive ourselves multiple times for the same mistake, we must recognize that healing takes time. It is essential to be patient with ourselves and honor our unique journeys. In this context, forgiveness becomes an ongoing practice rather than a destination.

Furthermore, forgiveness can extend beyond our personal experiences to encompass broader issues, such as forgiving others who have hurt us. While forgiving those who have wronged us can be challenging, it can also be liberating. Holding onto resentment can poison our emotional well-being, leading to bitterness and unhappiness. By choosing to forgive others, we free ourselves from the emotional burden of anger and resentment, allowing us to reclaim our inner peace. It is crucial to remember that forgiving someone does not mean condoning their actions; it simply means choosing to let go of the negative emotions associated with those actions.

As we explore the power of forgiveness, we can also consider practices that help facilitate this process. Mindfulness and meditation can be beneficial tools in cultivating forgiveness, allowing us to become aware of our emotions and release negativity. Guided meditations focused on forgiveness can help create a safe space for reflection and healing, enabling us to move through our feelings and find closure.

Forgiveness is a liberating practice that offers a path to freedom, particularly through self-forgiveness. By acknowledging our past mistakes, reflecting on the lessons learned, and practicing compassion toward ourselves, we can release the burdens that hold us back and embrace a brighter future. As we let go of resentment and anger—both toward ourselves and others—we open the door to healing, growth, and renewed connections. In the next chapter, we will explore the transformative power of gratitude and how cultivating an attitude of appreciation can further enrich our lives, strengthen our connections with others, and enhance our overall well-being. Together, we will learn to recognize the beauty in our experiences and foster a sense of fulfillment and joy.

25
COMPASSION IN TIMES OF FEAR

In times of fear and uncertainty, compassion emerges as a powerful antidote, offering both solace and strength to those who practice it. This chapter delves into how extending compassion to others can not only help alleviate our own fears but also inspire acts of bravery and resilience in the face of challenges. Through real-world examples, we will illustrate how empathy and kindness can lead to profound transformations, fostering a sense of community and courage even in the most daunting circumstances.

Fear can manifest in various forms—fear of the unknown, fear of failure, and fear of loss. During these trying times, we often find ourselves retreating into our own insecurities, feeling isolated and alone. However, when we turn our focus outward and cultivate compassion for others, we create a ripple effect that can uplift both ourselves and those around us. Compassion becomes a shared experience, connecting us through our common struggles and reminding us that we are not alone in our fears.

Consider the story of a teacher named Mr. Thompson, who worked in a school located in a neighborhood plagued by violence and instability. His students often came to class burdened by fear—fear for their safety, fear for their families, and fear for their futures. Recognizing the emotional toll this environment was taking on his students, Mr. Thompson decided to create a safe haven in his classroom. He encouraged open discussions about their fears, allowing students to express their feelings without judgment. Through this compassionate approach, Mr. Thompson not only helped his students process their emotions but also instilled in them the courage to face their challenges. His classroom became a space where empathy thrived, demonstrating how compassion can empower individuals to confront their fears collectively.

Another poignant example can be found in the aftermath of natural disasters, where communities often come together to support one another in times of crisis. When Hurricane Harvey struck Texas, thousands of residents found themselves displaced and fearful for their lives. In the face of this devastation, stories of compassion and bravery emerged as individuals stepped up to help their neighbors. One such story is that of a young woman named Maria, who, despite losing her own home, organized a local relief effort to provide food, clothing, and shelter to those affected. Her empathy fueled her actions, driving her to support others in their most vulnerable moments. Maria's bravery, inspired by her compassion for others, became a beacon of hope for her community, illustrating how acts of kindness can emerge even in the darkest times.

The act of giving and serving others can also be a powerful antidote to our own fears. Research has shown that engaging in acts of kindness not only benefits those we help but also boosts our own mental and emotional well-being. When we extend compassion to others, we shift our focus away from our fears, fostering a sense of purpose and connection. This principle is beautifully illustrated in the story of a man named James, who struggled with severe anxiety. He often found himself paralyzed by fear, unable to leave his home. In an effort to confront his anxiety, James began volunteering at a local homeless shelter. Through his interactions with those in need, he discovered that his compassion for others helped alleviate his own fears. By offering support and kindness to individuals facing dire circumstances, James found strength and resilience within himself, transforming his fear into a driving force for positive change.

Furthermore, compassion can serve as a catalyst for collective bravery. In moments of crisis, communities that foster empathy and support are better equipped to confront challenges together. During the COVID-19 pandemic, for example, many individuals faced fear and uncertainty regarding their health and safety. However, numerous acts of compassion emerged as neighbors checked in on one another, grocery stores provided free meals to healthcare workers, and communities organized virtual support groups. This collective compassion not only helped individuals feel less isolated in their fears but also inspired a sense of unity and resilience that transcended personal struggles. The bravery exhibited during these times was a testament to the power of empathy in overcoming adversity.

In addition to fostering personal growth and community resilience, compassion in times of fear also allows us to challenge our own biases and assumptions. When we approach others with empathy, we create opportunities for dialogue and understanding, breaking down barriers that often contribute to fear and division. For instance, in a diverse community where tensions exist among different cultural groups, initiatives that promote understanding through shared experiences can foster compassion and unity. By participating in community events that celebrate diversity and encourage dialogue, individuals can confront their fears and misconceptions, paving the way for a more inclusive and empathetic society.

To cultivate compassion in our own lives, we can begin by practicing active listening and empathy in our interactions with others. This involves being fully present and attentive to the feelings and experiences of those around us, allowing us to respond with kindness and understanding. Additionally, volunteering and engaging in community service can provide meaningful opportunities to connect with others and practice compassion. Whether through local organizations or informal acts of kindness, these experiences can help us build bridges and foster connections that transcend fear and isolation.

Compassion in times of fear serves as a powerful tool for personal and collective transformation. By extending empathy and kindness to others, we not only alleviate our own fears but also inspire acts of bravery that can change lives. Through the stories of individuals who have demonstrated courage inspired by compassion, we see that even in the darkest moments, there is potential for light and connection. As we embrace compassion, we foster a sense of community and resilience that empowers us to confront our fears together. In the next chapter, we will explore the theme of hope and how cultivating a hopeful mindset can further enrich our lives and guide us toward a brighter future. Together, we will learn to recognize and nurture the seeds of hope within ourselves and others, fostering a sense of possibility and purpose.

26

FINDING JOY IN HELPING OTHERS

In a world that often seems dominated by individualism and self-interest, the act of helping others stands as a beacon of hope and connection. This chapter explores the profound role that altruism plays in personal growth and fulfillment, illustrating how acts of kindness can not only transform the lives of those we help but also enrich our own lives in unexpected ways. Through inspiring examples and practical suggestions, readers will discover how finding joy in helping others can foster a deeper sense of purpose, belonging, and personal development.

At its core, altruism is rooted in empathy—the ability to understand and share the feelings of others. When we engage in acts of kindness, we tap into this innate sense of empathy, creating a bond that transcends our individual experiences. This connection can lead to a profound sense of joy and fulfillment, as we recognize the impact our actions have on the lives of others. Research has shown that helping others can trigger the release of endorphins in the brain, often referred to as the "helper's high." This natural boost in mood reinforces the idea that altruism is not just a selfless act; it can also be a source of personal happiness and satisfaction.

Consider the story of Maya, a young woman who struggled with feelings of loneliness and disconnection after moving to a new city. Initially, she found it challenging to make friends and often felt isolated. In an effort to find purpose and connection, Maya decided to volunteer at a local animal shelter. Each week, she dedicated her time to caring for the animals, walking dogs, and helping with adoption events. As she poured her heart into her volunteer work, Maya discovered a deep sense of joy in helping others—both the animals she cared for and the families she assisted in finding their new pets. Through this experience, she not only found fulfillment but also built lasting friendships with fellow volunteers, creating a supportive community that enriched her life.

The joy derived from helping others extends beyond individual experiences; it can also foster a sense of belonging and connection within our communities. When we engage in acts of kindness, we contribute to the greater good, creating a ripple effect that can inspire others to do the same. This collective sense of purpose strengthens social bonds and promotes a culture of compassion and empathy. A compelling example can be found in community initiatives, such as neighborhood clean-up days or food drives, where individuals come together to serve a common goal. In these instances, the act of helping others fosters camaraderie and connection, reinforcing the idea that we are all part of something larger than ourselves.

Moreover, acts of altruism can provide a profound sense of perspective, helping us appreciate our own circumstances while fostering gratitude. When we engage in helping those who may be struggling, we often gain insight into our own lives, recognizing the privileges we may take for granted. This perspective shift can cultivate a greater sense of empathy and understanding, allowing us to approach life with a renewed appreciation for the interconnectedness of our experiences. For example, a group of students from a local high school organized a fundraiser to support families affected by a recent disaster. As they learned about the challenges these families faced, they gained a deeper appreciation for their own lives, ultimately leading to a stronger commitment to community service and advocacy.

To harness the joy of helping others, readers are encouraged to explore various avenues for altruism in their own lives. Volunteering is a powerful way to connect with others while making a meaningful impact in the community. This could involve serving at a local food bank, mentoring youth, or participating in environmental conservation efforts. However, altruism doesn't always require a formal commitment; small, everyday acts of kindness can also have a significant impact. Whether it's helping a neighbor with groceries, offering a listening ear to a friend in need, or donating to a charity, these gestures foster connection and bring joy to both the giver and the recipient.

Engaging in acts of kindness also allows us to cultivate new skills and passions. Volunteering can open doors to new experiences and opportunities, providing avenues for personal growth that we may not have encountered otherwise. For instance, someone who volunteers to teach art classes to children may discover a newfound passion for teaching or creativity. Similarly, an individual who participates in community gardening may develop a deeper connection to nature and sustainability. By stepping outside our comfort zones and engaging in altruistic endeavors, we can discover hidden talents and interests that enrich our lives.

Additionally, it's essential to recognize that the joy of helping others is not limited to grand gestures; it can be found in the simplicity of daily interactions. Acts of kindness, no matter how small, contribute to a culture of compassion and positivity. A smile to a stranger, a compliment to a coworker, or a thank-you note to a friend can all create ripples of joy and connection. By incorporating these small acts into our daily routines, we cultivate a mindset of gratitude and generosity, transforming our outlook on life.

Finding joy in helping others is a powerful catalyst for personal growth and fulfillment. Through acts of altruism, we can foster connections, gain perspective, and discover newfound passions that enrich our lives. The stories of individuals who have experienced joy through helping others remind us of the inherent power of compassion and empathy. As we embark on our own journeys of altruism, we not only uplift those around us but also cultivate a deeper sense of purpose and belonging within ourselves. In the next chapter, we will explore the theme of hope, examining how cultivating a hopeful mindset can further enhance our lives and inspire us to pursue our dreams. Together, we will learn to nurture the seeds of hope within ourselves and others, fostering a sense of possibility and resilience in our lives.

27

BUILDING A SUPPORT NETWORK

In our journey through fears and dreams, the importance of surrounding ourselves with a supportive network of individuals cannot be overstated. This chapter discusses how a well-nurtured support network can serve as a foundation for personal growth, resilience, and bravery. Readers will explore the benefits of building meaningful relationships with like-minded individuals and learn practical strategies for cultivating these connections in their own lives.

At the heart of a strong support network is the idea of shared understanding and empathy. When we surround ourselves with people who resonate with our experiences and aspirations, we create an environment that fosters growth and courage. These supportive relationships can provide encouragement during challenging times, celebrate our successes, and hold us accountable as we strive to reach our goals. A support network can act as a safety net, reminding us that we are not alone in our struggles and that there are others who believe in our potential.

Consider the story of Alex, a young entrepreneur who dreamed of starting his own business. At first, he felt isolated in his ambitions, unsure of how to navigate the challenges that lay ahead. After attending a local networking event, he met several individuals who shared his passion for entrepreneurship. By forming connections with these like-minded individuals, Alex discovered a wealth of knowledge, support, and encouragement. They became a sounding board for his ideas, offered constructive feedback, and celebrated his milestones. With this network behind him, Alex felt emboldened to take risks and pursue his dream, knowing that he had a community cheering him on.

The process of building a support network begins with self-awareness and clarity about what we seek in our relationships. It's essential to identify the qualities we value in others and the types of support we need to thrive. Are we looking for mentors who can guide us? Peers who can share similar experiences? Friends who uplift us during difficult times? By reflecting on our needs, we can set intentions for the connections we wish to cultivate. This clarity allows us to seek out individuals who align with our values and aspirations, making it easier to form meaningful relationships.

Once we've identified what we're looking for, it's time to take proactive steps to connect with others. This can involve attending community events, joining interest-based clubs or organizations, or participating in online forums related to our passions. For instance, someone interested in writing may join a local writers' group or an online platform where aspiring authors can share their work and support one another. These environments provide fertile ground for nurturing connections, as they bring together individuals who share common interests and goals. Engaging in these spaces opens doors to new friendships and opportunities that may not have been accessible otherwise.

As we build our support network, it's vital to approach these relationships with authenticity and openness. Vulnerability is often a prerequisite for meaningful connections, as it allows others to see us for who we truly are. Sharing our fears, aspirations, and challenges fosters trust and encourages reciprocity in our relationships. When we show up authentically, we invite others to do the same, creating a space for genuine connection and mutual support.

Additionally, nurturing these relationships requires effort and commitment. Just as we invest time in our personal growth, we must also invest in the people who lift us up. Regular check-ins, supportive messages, and celebrating each other's successes go a long way in strengthening our bonds. For example, organizing monthly meet-ups with our support network can provide a platform for sharing experiences, seeking advice, and fostering a sense of community. These gatherings not only reinforce connections but also create a space for collective growth and accountability.

It's also important to remember that a support network is not solely about receiving support; it's about giving as well. The act of being there for others can be equally fulfilling, as it allows us to contribute to someone else's journey. By offering encouragement, sharing our insights, and lending a listening ear, we reinforce our own connections and foster a culture of support within our network. This mutual exchange of support creates a cycle of positivity, where individuals feel empowered to face their fears and pursue their dreams.

As we navigate our personal journeys, it's essential to be open to evolving relationships. Our needs and goals may change over time, and it's natural for some connections to shift or fade. This does not diminish the value of those relationships but rather allows us to make space for new connections that align more closely with our current aspirations. Embracing this fluidity enables us to create a dynamic support network that adapts to our growth and evolving circumstances.

Building a supportive network of like-minded individuals is crucial for personal growth and the pursuit of our dreams. By surrounding ourselves with people who understand our journeys and share our values, we create a foundation of encouragement and accountability. Through self-awareness, proactive engagement, and authenticity, we can cultivate meaningful relationships that inspire bravery and resilience. As we invest in nurturing these connections, we not only uplift ourselves but also contribute to the collective growth of our community. In the next chapter, we will explore the transformative power of hope, examining how cultivating a hopeful mindset can guide us through challenges and inspire us to pursue our dreams with renewed vigor. Together, we will learn to nurture hope within ourselves and others, fostering a sense of possibility and purpose in our lives.

28

CHOOSING KINDNESS EVERY DAY

In the fast-paced world we live in, where challenges and distractions often vie for our attention, the simple yet profound act of kindness can easily be overlooked. This chapter emphasizes the incredible value of everyday kindness, illustrating how even the smallest gestures can have a transformative impact on our lives and the lives of others. Readers are encouraged to view kindness not only as an essential aspect of our humanity but also as a reflection of courage—an intentional choice that can uplift both ourselves and those around us.

Kindness can take many forms, from a warm smile to a stranger to a thoughtful note for a friend. These acts, though seemingly minor, create ripples of positivity that extend far beyond the initial moment. Research has shown that engaging in acts of kindness can lead to increased feelings of happiness and fulfillment, reinforcing the idea that kindness is a powerful tool for enhancing our emotional well-being. When we choose to be kind, we engage in a reciprocal relationship with ourselves and the world, fostering connections that enrich our lives.

Consider the story of Sarah, a busy mother of three who often found herself overwhelmed by daily responsibilities. One day, as she rushed through the grocery store, she noticed an elderly man struggling to reach for an item on a high shelf. Despite her hectic schedule, Sarah felt a surge of compassion and approached the man, offering to help. Their brief interaction turned into a delightful conversation, and Sarah left the store feeling lighter and more connected to her community. This small act of kindness not only brightened the man's day but also brought Sarah a sense of joy and fulfillment, reminding her of the power of kindness in everyday life.

Moreover, kindness can serve as a powerful antidote to fear and negativity. In moments of uncertainty, offering kindness to others can create a sense of safety and connection. When we extend compassion to those around us, we cultivate an environment where people feel valued and seen, fostering resilience in both ourselves and others. For instance, during difficult times, such as natural disasters or community crises, acts of kindness become even more vital. Neighbors helping neighbors, sharing resources, and offering emotional support create a web of solidarity that can help individuals navigate fear and uncertainty with greater strength.

In practicing kindness, we not only uplift others but also nurture our own courage. It can be intimidating to reach out and offer help, especially if we fear rejection or are uncertain about how our actions will be received. However, by choosing kindness, we step outside of our comfort zones and confront these fears head-on. Each act of kindness requires a degree of vulnerability—whether it's complimenting a colleague, offering assistance, or simply being present for a friend in need. By embracing this vulnerability, we grow in our ability to connect with others and cultivate a deeper sense of courage.

To integrate kindness into our daily lives, it can be helpful to cultivate a mindset that prioritizes small, intentional actions. This could involve setting a daily intention to perform one act of kindness, no matter how minor it may seem. For example, holding the door open for someone, sending a heartfelt message, or expressing gratitude to a loved one are all small acts that can significantly impact someone's day. These moments of kindness not only bring joy to others but also create a positive feedback loop, enhancing our own sense of fulfillment and connection.

Additionally, we can look for opportunities to practice kindness in our routines and interactions. Whether at work, school, or in our communities, we can challenge ourselves to be more aware of the needs of those around us. This may involve actively listening to a coworker who seems overwhelmed, offering words of encouragement to a friend facing challenges, or simply making eye contact and smiling at those we pass on the street. These moments of connection, though small, have the power to remind us of our shared humanity and the importance of uplifting one another.

Kindness can also be a tool for fostering resilience in challenging times. When we face adversity, reaching out to help others can provide a sense of purpose and perspective. For instance, volunteering for a local charity or participating in community service projects can shift our focus away from our own struggles and allow us to contribute positively to the lives of others. In doing so, we not only support those in need but also cultivate a sense of agency and strength within ourselves.

Choosing kindness every day is a powerful practice that enriches our lives and the lives of others. Through small acts of kindness, we can foster connection, cultivate courage, and create a ripple effect of positivity in our communities. As we embrace the value of everyday kindness, we remind ourselves that each gesture—no matter how small—has the potential to uplift and transform. By prioritizing kindness in our interactions, we cultivate a mindset that nurtures our own well-being while contributing to a more compassionate world. In the next chapter, we will explore the theme of gratitude, examining how cultivating a grateful mindset can further enhance our lives and strengthen our connections with others. Together, we will learn to recognize and appreciate the abundance that surrounds us, fostering a sense of joy and fulfillment in our journey.

29
LIVING AUTHENTICALLY WITH PURPOSE

Living authentically is more than just a trend or a buzzword; it is a profound commitment to align our actions, values, and beliefs with our true selves. This chapter explores the significance of authenticity and purpose in our lives, emphasizing that the courage to live authentically is a lifelong practice. As we navigate our dreams and fears, embracing our authentic selves allows us to cultivate a sense of fulfillment and meaning in our lives.

At its core, living authentically means being true to who we are, recognizing our unique strengths, passions, and values. It requires a deep level of self-awareness, as we must first understand what authenticity looks like for us individually. This process often involves reflecting on our experiences, desires, and the influences that have shaped us. By taking the time to explore our inner selves, we can gain clarity on what truly matters to us, allowing us to set intentions that align with our authentic identities.

Consider the journey of Lisa, a talented artist who spent years conforming to societal expectations of what success should look like. For a long time, she pursued a corporate career that did not resonate with her passion for creativity. The pressure to fit into a conventional mold led Lisa to suppress her artistic talents, resulting in a growing sense of disconnection and dissatisfaction. However, after a period of reflection, she realized that living authentically meant embracing her passion for art, even if it defied societal norms. With courage, Lisa made the leap to pursue her dream, dedicating herself to her craft and finding fulfillment in creating art that reflected her true self.

As we embark on our own journeys toward authenticity, it is essential to recognize that the path is not always linear. Fear and self-doubt often arise when we challenge the status quo and seek to live authentically. We may worry about the judgments of others or fear the uncertainty that comes with pursuing our true passions. However, it is precisely in these moments of vulnerability that we cultivate the courage necessary to honor our authentic selves. Embracing our fears allows us to navigate the complexities of our identities and fosters resilience as we confront obstacles along the way.

To support our journey toward living authentically, we can practice self-compassion and patience. It is important to remember that authenticity is not a destination but rather an ongoing process of growth and self-discovery. We may encounter setbacks and moments of doubt, but these experiences are valuable opportunities for learning and reflection. By treating ourselves with kindness during challenging times, we create a nurturing environment that encourages exploration and growth. This compassionate approach empowers us to embrace our true selves, even in the face of adversity.

Aligning our actions with our values also requires a commitment to intentional decision-making. As we clarify what is meaningful to us, we can begin to make choices that reflect our authentic selves. This may involve setting boundaries, pursuing new opportunities, or letting go of relationships that no longer serve us. For example, someone who values environmental sustainability may choose to advocate for eco-friendly practices in their workplace or community. By making decisions that align with our values, we reinforce our commitment to living authentically and purposefully.

Moreover, sharing our authentic selves with others can inspire those around us to do the same. When we embrace vulnerability and authenticity, we create spaces for open dialogue and connection. Our courage to express our true selves can encourage others to reflect on their own identities and aspirations, fostering a culture of authenticity within our communities. Through storytelling and sharing our experiences, we can build bridges of understanding and create an environment that honors individuality and courage.

Living authentically also involves embracing our unique journeys and recognizing that there is no one "right" way to pursue our dreams. Each of us has our own path, shaped by our experiences, passions, and values. By reframing our perspective on success and fulfillment, we can shift away from external validation and focus on what truly resonates with our authentic selves. This mindset allows us to celebrate our individuality and find joy in our unique contributions to the world.

As we strive to live authentically with purpose, it is essential to cultivate resilience in the face of challenges. There will inevitably be moments when we encounter obstacles or setbacks that test our commitment to our authentic selves. During these times, it can be helpful to reconnect with our values and aspirations, reminding ourselves of the reasons we embarked on this journey. Practicing mindfulness and reflection can also provide clarity and grounding as we navigate difficulties, helping us maintain our sense of purpose and authenticity.

Living authentically with purpose is a courageous and lifelong practice that requires self-awareness, vulnerability, and intentionality. By aligning our actions with our values and embracing our true selves, we can cultivate a sense of fulfillment and meaning in our lives. As we navigate our dreams and fears, we honor both our aspirations and our authentic identities, creating a rich tapestry of experiences that reflect who we are. In the final chapter, we will explore the theme of integration, examining how we can weave together the lessons learned throughout our journey into a cohesive and empowered narrative that propels us toward a fulfilling future. Together, we will celebrate the beauty of our unique journeys and embrace the possibility of becoming the bravest versions of ourselves.

30

THE BRAVEST ME - EMBRACING THE JOURNEY FORWARD

As we reach the culmination of "The Bravest Me: A Journey Through Fears and Dreams," it's essential to take a moment to reflect on the transformative journey you have embarked upon. Throughout these pages, you have explored the intricate interplay of courage, curiosity, and compassion—three guiding forces that empower you to navigate the complexities of life. This final chapter celebrates your growth and encourages you to embrace the journey ahead with an open heart and mind.

At the heart of this journey is the recognition that bravery is not the absence of fear, but rather the willingness to face it. Each chapter has illuminated the unique fears that can anchor us, from the shadows of doubt and the weight of past traumas to the daunting specter of rejection. However, you have also discovered the remarkable capacity for growth that lies within these challenges. By confronting your fears with courage, you have begun to break free from the limitations that once held you back. This newfound strength is a testament to your resilience and determination to live a life that reflects your true self.

Curiosity has served as a powerful catalyst for change throughout your journey. By choosing to ask questions, seek knowledge, and embrace new experiences, you have expanded your horizons and unlocked the potential for growth and self-discovery. Remember that curiosity is a lifelong companion on this journey; it invites you to explore the world with wonder and openness. As you move forward, allow your curiosity to guide you toward new opportunities and possibilities, reminding you that every experience—both joyous and challenging—contributes to the richness of your life.

Compassion, both for yourself and others, has been a cornerstone of your journey. It is through acts of kindness, understanding, and empathy that you create connections that uplift and inspire. As you continue to cultivate compassion in your relationships, remember that it has the power to heal wounds, bridge divides, and foster a sense of belonging. Your ability to empathize with the struggles of others not only nurtures your connections but also reinforces your commitment to creating a more compassionate world.

As you reflect on the courage you have developed, acknowledge the growth that comes from vulnerability. Embracing vulnerability allows you to share your authentic self with the world, inviting others to do the same. It is in these moments of honesty that deep connections are formed, fostering a sense of community and support. The courage to be vulnerable is a lifelong practice, one that will continue to shape your relationships and experiences as you journey forward.

With the lessons learned throughout this book, you are now equipped to shape a future that resonates with your authentic self. The courage to question the status quo, pursue your dreams, and challenge your fears will guide you as you navigate the uncertainties of life. Embrace the notion that your path may not always be linear; there will be ups and downs, but each experience is an opportunity for growth and learning. Trust in your ability to adapt and evolve, knowing that every step you take is part of a larger journey toward self-fulfillment.

In this chapter, we celebrate the culmination of your journey, but also the beginning of a new chapter in your life. Carry with you the lessons of self-compassion, courage, and curiosity as you forge ahead. Allow your dreams to be your compass, guiding you toward a future filled with purpose and passion. Remember that you are not alone on this journey—there are countless others who share your aspirations and struggles. By connecting with like-minded individuals and nurturing a supportive network, you can continue to grow and inspire each other as you navigate the complexities of life together.

As you embrace the journey forward, take time to reflect on the vision you have for your future. What dreams do you wish to pursue? What values will guide your actions? Allow your heart and mind to dream big, and remember that every small step you take brings you closer to realizing your aspirations. Embrace the courage to step outside your comfort zone, the curiosity to explore new possibilities, and the compassion to uplift yourself and others along the way.

In conclusion, "The Bravest Me" is not merely a destination but an ongoing journey—a lifelong exploration of fears and dreams, courage and curiosity, compassion and connection. You have the power to shape your future, to embrace each moment with authenticity, and to honor both your dreams and fears. As you step into this new chapter, may you continue to embody the bravery that resides within you and inspire those around you to do the same. Your journey is uniquely yours, and it is filled with endless possibilities waiting to be discovered. Embrace it with open arms, and remember that you are indeed the bravest version of yourself.

147 The Bravest Me: A Journey Through Fears and Dreams

148 The Bravest Me: A Journey Through Fears and Dreams

ABOUT THE AUTHOR

Laura Lee is a passionate author and speaker, born and raised in a small town where the values of community and resilience were instilled in her from a young age. Her upbringing in a close-knit environment sparked her curiosity about the world and the human experience, shaping her desire to inspire others through the written word.

With a background in personal development, Laura has dedicated her life to exploring the intersections of courage, compassion, and authenticity. Her journey through fears and dreams has led her to uncover the transformative power of self-discovery and emotional resilience, themes that resonate deeply in her work.